In Pursuit of God

By

Francine E. Shaw

Published by
ACTS Publishing

© 2017 Francine E. Shaw

Published by:
ACTS Publishing
P.O. Box 03600
Highland Park, MI 48203

All Scripture quotations, unless otherwise indicated, are taken from The King James Version (KJV) of the Bible copyright © 1994 by Zondervan

Bold comments within brackets noted in scripture are emphasis added by author. Take note that the name satan and associated names are not capitalized. We choose not to give him any preeminence, even to the point of violating grammatical rules.

Author: Francine E. Shaw
Cover Design: ACTS Creative Team
Editor: ACTS Editorial Team

First U.S. edition Year 2017
Publisher's Cataloging-In-Publication Data

Shaw, Francine E.

In Pursuit of God
Biblical principles and practices for victorious Christian Living

10 Digit ISBN   09861767-2-9   Perfect Bound Soft Cover
13 Digit ISBN   978-0-9861767-2-2   Perfect Bound Soft Cover

1.   Christianity, Christian Living

For current information about releases by Francine E. Shaw or other releases contact: *ACTS Publishing*, P. O. Box 03600, Highland Park, MI 48203

Printed in the United States of America

V1. 01 16 2017

Dedicated

To the All Wise God, my Father, the Creator of all mankind

To Jesus Christ my Savior, and LORD

To the Holy Spirit, who has empowered me
to walk and live in the Spirit.

To my Pop, Tenzly Turner Sr.

To my Father Robert Perry, and Mother Ella Turner
who are both in the presence of the LORD.
Thank you for bringing me into the world.

To my Husband Ronald G. Shaw
who has supported me throughout my Journey.

To my Daughters, Katrina K. Lyman-Pittman,
Felicia A. Gayle and Karimeh M. Lyman

To my Son-in-laws, Anthony Pittman, and Donald Gayle

To my Grandchildren, Anthony Pittman, Donovan Gayle,
Doshanay Lyman, and Anna Pittman

To all of my Uncles and Aunts (Living and deceased)

To all of my Sister and Brothers
Especially Barbara Ann and Willie J. Lyman
(both deceased)

To all my Nieces and Nephews
(living and deceased)

To Pastor Lernard Goggans Sr.
and my New World Community Church Family

Thank all of you for molding and shaping me throughout
our many Joys and Sorrows!

In Pursuit of God

By

Francine E. Shaw

Table of contents

In Pursuit of God

-Preface-

In Pursuit of God is the third in a series of teachings geared toward helping the believer whose desire is to grow spiritually mature in the Lord. We grow mature spiritually by understanding and implementing the word of God in our lives. *In Pursuit of God* will show you how to pursue God with all your heart.

The Apostle Paul, in his letter to the church at Ephesus wrote these words: *"Wherefore I also, after I heard of your faith in the Lord Jesus, and love unto all the saints. Cease not to give thanks for you. making mention of you in my prayers; That the God of our Lord Jesus Christ, the Father of glory, may give unto you the spirit of wisdom, and revelation in the knowledge of him: The eyes of your understanding being enlightened; that ye may know what is the hope of his calling, and what is the riches of the glory of his inheritance in the saints* (Ephesians 1:15-18)."

The Apostle Paul in his prayer to God asks that the saints at Ephesus be given the spirit of wisdom and the spirit of revelation in the knowledge of Jesus Christ. His prayer also was for God to enlighten their eyes of understanding to enable them to see, perceive and or to understand spiritual things or the spiritual things of God, so that they would know the hope of their calling and the riches of the glory of Christ's inheritance in the saints. This also is my prayer for you!

Wisdom and discernment are both gifts (1 Corinthians 12:1-11) and are given to the believer for the sole purpose of growing spiritually mature. The word of God not only allows us to hear what is said, it also allows us to see what is being said. God enlightens our eyes of understanding through the gift of discernment. It is called insight and it is the apprehension into the nature of things. To apprehend, is to understand. The word of God allows us to become conscious or sensible of any given subject pertaining to life.

Unlike, *Wisdom for Financial Success from a Biblical*

In Pursuit of God

Perspective and *The Cycle of Sin*, this book was birth out of much toil over the fact, that so many are being misled by those whose pernicious ways are being followed and through covetousness the scripture says with feigned words are being made merchandise of (2 Peter 2:1-3). These false prophets and teachers are themselves deceived and are deceiving many in believing they can become prosperous, remain in sin and still inherit the kingdom of God. Rather than the church impacting the world, the world has impacted the church.

The Apostle Paul in Galatians 5:19-21 says:

*"Now the works of the flesh are manifest, which are these; Adultery, fornication, uncleanness, lasciviousness, idolatry, witchcraft, hatred, variance, emulation, wrath, strife, seditions, heresies, envyings, murders, drunkenness, revellings, and such like of which I tell you before, as I have also told you in time past, that they which do such things **shall not inherit the kingdom of God**."*

What do we not understand? The Apostle Paul is not giving warning to the world, but to the church. He goes on to say in Ephesians 4:17-21:

*"This I say therefore, and testify in the Lord, that ye henceforth walk not as other Gentiles walk, in the vanity of their minds, **Having the understanding darkened**, being alienated from the **life of God through ignorance** that is in them, because of the **blindness of their heart**: Who being pass feeling have given themselves over unto lasciviousness, (given to or expressing lust) to work all uncleanness (morally defiled) with greediness (excessively desirous of acquiring or possessing). But ye have not so learned Christ; if so be that ye heard him, and have been **taught by him**, as **the** truth is in Jesus: (John 14:6)."*

Wisdom for Financial Success from a Biblical Perspective and *The Cycle on Sin* were both written also to help believers become more aware of why remaining in sin can cause us to be off course in our walk with the LORD and why so many believers are yet seeking the things which are seen and temporal, rather than the things that are unseen and eternal. Both books were written to help believers to identify the spiritual warfare we are engaged in (Revelation 12:7-12) and that we not only need the wisdom of God in our finances to become financially successful. But, we need discernment to live also godly lives.

In Pursuit of God was written to show the believer how having an understanding of forgiveness, giving, prayer and fasting along with love and joy is essential to our spiritual growth and how having an understanding of why it's so important for us to grow mature spiritually will greatly contribute to our growth progression.

The intent of this book is to show how you can pursue God through the three spiritual tools given us to exercise our faith in God and how through several of the fruit of the Spirit, we are able to walk in the newness of life. It is my prayer and desire for God to enlighten your eyes of understanding and to give you the spirit of wisdom and revelation into the knowledge of His Son, Jesus Christ. My challenge is for you to seek the LORD with all your heart.

"And ye shall seek me, and find me, when ye shall search for me with all your heart." (Jeremiah 29:13)

Repent for the Kingdom of God is at hand!

In Pursuit of God

___Introduction___

Life pursuing God is an activity that one engages in and it requires special training and skills. It is a journey where we discover who we truly are only while walking in the right direction. We all are in pursuit of something or someone. It can be an education, a career, or a marriage. It can be a dream, vision or happiness. It can be a relationship or just seeking after wealth. What are you pursuing?

There are really only two things in life you and I can pursue after. We are either pursuing after God or after mammon which is the personification of wealth or worldly possessions and it is God's chief competitor. Everything we do leads to one or the other. Jesus let us know that: *"No man can serve two masters: for either he will hate the one, and love the other, or else he will hold to the one, and despise* (reject) *the other. Ye cannot serve God and mammon* (Matthew 6:24).*"*

The people of God today have the same problem that Israel had centuries ago. Rather than becoming submissive to the will of God, they became disobedient and were compromising God's way of life. They were serving God with lip service and not with heart service. Jesus in Matthew 15:8 said: *"This people draweth nigh unto me with their mouth, and honoureth me with their lips; but their heart is far from me."* The children of Israel were not following the instructions given them of God. They were living according to their own will rather than the will of God.

The generations to come will be saved. But we, the people of God must obey Him. We must begin to live holy lives teaching our children and grandchildren children from birth to adulthood the ways of God.

In Jeremiah chapter twenty nine, the LORD allowed the children of Israel to be taken into captivity because of their disobedience. Yet, while in captivity they were given the instructions to build houses to dwell in. They were to plant gardens to eat from them, and to take unto themselves wives and to bear children and their sons and daughters were to take to themselves wives and husbands to bear children so that they would increase and not diminish.

Instructions were also given for them to seek peace and to pray unto the LORD for peace, so that they would live in peace among the heathens. Israel was told not to believe their own dreams which they have dreamed nor believe the diviners or the prophets because they were prophesying lies that their captivity would be only several years (Jeremiah 27:14-15; 28:1-17).

In other words, they were to repent and become obedient to the LORD in their captive state. We too must repent and become obedient for in our obedience are we able to walk in our deliverance. We must repent and turn completely toward God.

The Prophet Jeremiah was told by the LORD to speak unto the people of God these words saying: *"For thus saith the LORD, That after seventy years be accomplished at Babylon I will visit you, and perform my good word toward you, in causing you to return to this place. For I know the thoughts that I think toward you, saith the LORD, thoughts of peace, and not of evil, to give you an expected end* (hope and a future). *Then shall ye call upon me, and ye shall go and pray unto me, and I will hearken unto you. And ye shall seek me, and find me, when ye shall search for me with all your heart* (Jeremiah 29:10-13)."

The LORD indicates that after seventy years of following the instruction given them. They then were to call upon Him by praying, seeking and searching after Him with all their heart.

The heart in this context is interchangeable with the mind. Scripture says: *"For as he thinketh in his heart so is he:* (Proverbs 23:7a; Matthew 5:19)." Knowledge of the mind is found to consist of the intellect, the emotions and the will. The children of Israel were instructed to search for the LORD with all of their intellect, their emotions and their will.

We can no longer seek the LORD with half our hearts. This is exactly what we do when we refuse to separate ourselves from the world. We want to hold on to the old while trying to live in the newness of life (Romans 6:4). It is impossible. Why? We are a new creation in Christ Jesus, old things are passed away; all things are become new (2 Corinthians 5:17).

If we are going to change our behavior, we must realize that our perception and our perspective on life must change also. In order to become obedient to the will of God, we must understand what God is saying. Perception is insight. The ability or capacity to perceive and perceive means to obtain knowledge of through the senses; to see, hear and feel. Perspective on the other hand, is a mental view or outlook; the way something is viewed by the mind.

In growing spiritually mature. We learn to view life through the written word of God. Therefore, you and I must renew our minds through the truth of God's word (Matthew 4:4; Romans 12:1-3). This will never happen if we do not set time aside to read, study and to meditate in the word of God (2 Timothy 3:14-17; 2 Timothy 2:15; Psalms 1:1-3). Proverbs 13:15 says: *"Good understanding giveth favour: but the way of the transgressor is* (difficult) *hard."*

Favour means to help or to facilitate; and to facilitate means, to make easier; to assist the progress of (growth). The transgressor's way is hard (difficult) simply because he or she being citizens of the Kingdom of God, are transgressing the commands (rules that governs us) of God (Acts 9:5-6).

David in Psalms 51:12-13, makes a distinction between the sinner and the transgressor when he says:

In Pursuit of God

"Restore unto me the joy of thy salvation; and uphold me with thy free spirit. ***Then will I teach transgressors thy ways; and sinners shall be converted unto thee.****"* This was my prayer to God.

We must first be taught the truth of God's word and in being taught we must then gradually implement it in our lives. We must implement the truth which means to use it to do the work in us. In order for us to walk in our deliverance (Colossians 1:12-14; John 8:30-32). We must walk by faith, faith in the word of God (Hebrews 11:1, 6). Truth is absolute, which means perfect, having no defects or faults: flawless; accurate, absolute. 2 Samuel 22:31-33 says:

"As for God, his way (straight and narrow) *is perfect; the word of the LORD is* (proven) *tried: he is a* (shield) *buckler to all them that trust in him. For who is God, save* (except) *the LORD? And who is a rock, save our God? God is my strength and power: and he maketh my way perfect."* Scripture goes on to say:

"There is a way (broad and wide) *which seemeth right unto a man, but the end thereof are the ways of death* (Proverbs 14:12).*"*

The LORD has given us three spiritual tools to help us to develop discipline and self-control and in our development of discipline and self-control. We learn to obey God intentionally. Intent is having the intellect, emotions and will focus on a specific purpose and that purpose is to obey God. The devil's intent is to lure us into sin by tempting us with foolish living, worldly possessions, pleasure and wealth. Rather than seeking after worldly possessions, pleasure and wealth, Jesus tells us:

"But seek ye first the kingdom of God, and his righteousness; And all these things shall be added unto you (Matthew 6:33).*"*

4

-Introduction-

God wants us to pursue Him and not pursue after worldly possessions, pleasure and wealth. God is calling us to live wisely. Why? Because, God loves us and love is what everyone is seeking after, but in all the wrong places.

Therefore, if we have an understanding of how sin and money influences us it will greatly contribute to us becoming obedient. *Wisdom for Financial Success from a Biblical Perspective, The Cycle of Sin* and *In Pursuit of God* are all available now on www.amazon.com, an investment that will change your life. If you have not received Jesus as your Savior and want to become saved, pray this prayer sincerely from your heart:

PRAYER FOR SALVATION,

Heavenly Father,

I come to you in the Name of your only begotten Son, Jesus Christ. Romans 10:13 says: *"whosoever shall call upon the name of the Lord shall be saved."* I am calling on your Name Jesus, to save me!

I believe you died on the cross for my sins, were buried and on the third day God raised you from the dead and now you are sitting at the right hand of the Father interceding for me.

Jesus, I am asking you to come into my heart, and to take full control of my life. Help me become the person you are calling me to be. I repent of my sins and surrender my heart totally and completely to you. Forgive me for all of my sins and cleanse me from my unrighteousness. I accept and confess you as my LORD and Savior. Thank you for coming into my heart and sealing me to the day of redemption. Thank you for forgiving me of my sins and making your home in my heart. In Jesus' Name I pray. Amen! So be it!

5

In Pursuit of God

___Chapter 1___

In Pursuit of God

"And ye shall seek me, and find me,
when ye shall search for me,
with all your heart."
Jeremiah 29:13

Life is a pursuit. Pursuit defined, is the act of pursuing, chasing, striding after something or someone; an effort to secure, attain, a quest.

It is vitally important that we understand first and foremost that everything stems from our hearts. Matthew 15:18, lets us know that it is not what goes into the mouth that defiles a man. But, what proceeds out of the heart; it defile a man. The Apostle Paul continues to explain the heart by saying "with the heart man believes unto righteousness and with the mouth confession is made unto salvation" (Romans 10:9; 1 John 1:9). Therefore, we are told to "*guard* (or to keep) *our heart with all diligence for out of it are the issues of life* (Proverbs 4:23)." Issues are subjects of concern, a source of conflict, misgiving, or emotional distress.

Issues that are not dealt with or are unresolved will lay dominant in our hearts, and when triggered (or tricked) will surface. It is what we call displaced emotions or aggression and over a period of time if accumulated will cause us to say or do something we otherwise would not have done if we were not angry. Aggression is the destruction we see in the world today, unprovoked hostility. Anger is a wile of the devil and satan's evil forces will take hold of anger and ruin the very life of those who open that door to sin. Ephesians 4:26 says:

"Be ye angry, and sin not: let not the sun go down upon your wrath: Neither give place (opportunity) *to the devil."*

In Pursuit of God

Man is tribune which means he has three parts which consists of the spirit, the soul (mind) and body. What is the heart? The heart is our inner most being. It is the part of us which think, feels and acts. It is the part God wants us to surrender. The mind and soul are the same and according to scriptures, is our heart (Matthew 15:18; Proverbs 23:7a).

The Prophet Isaiah says: *"Seek ye the LORD while he may be found, call upon him while he is near: Let the wicked forsake his way, and the unrighteous man his thoughts: and Let him return unto the LORD, and he will have mercy upon him: and to our God, for he will abundantly pardon* (Isaiah 55:6-7).*"*

God is calling us to return unto the LORD (Malachi 3:7-12; Matthew 11:28-30) and unto Him for He will forgive and abundantly pardon us.

God has provided a way for us to be reconciled to Himself through the shed blood of Jesus Christ, who is the Lamb of God. Jesus has redeemed and has restored us back to our rightful place in God and has given us back the right to the tree of life. Those of us who are in Christ and are born of the Spirit of God because of the new birth not only can hear what God is saying. But, we can see also what God is saying with the renewing of our mind (Romans 12:2) We are able then to glimpse at the tree of life now in heaven and have hope and a future.

For the Apostle John said: *"And (Jesus) he shewed me a pure river of water of life, clear as crystal, proceeding out of the throne of God and of the Lamb. In the midst of the street of it, and on either side of the river, was there the tree of life, which bare twelve manner of fruits, and yielded her fruit every month, and the leaves of the tree were for the healing of the nations. And there shall be no more curse. but the throne of God and of the Lamb shall be in it; and **his servants** shall **serve** him* (Revelation 22:1-3).*"*

Keep in mind that all of mankind was curse because Adam and Eve disobeyed the personal commandment of God not to eat from the tree of the knowledge of good and evil that was in the midst of the Garden of Eden. And because of their disobedience we inherited their sin (Romans 3:23) and at birth were spiritually dead. But God, who is great in mercy have reconciled and restored us back to Himself through Jesus Christ's obedience.

We are told in Romans 5:14-15, 19, *"Nevertheless death reigned from Adam to Moses, even over them that had not sinned after the similitude of Adam's transgression, who is the figure of him that was to come. But not as the offence, so also is the free gift. For if through the offence of one many be dead, much more the grace of God, and the gift by grace, which is by one man, Jesus Christ, hath abounded unto many. For as by one man's disobedience many were made sinners, so by the obedience of one shall many **be made righteous**."*

We pursue God by seeking the truth and by understanding that His word is His will. We are now under the New Testament Covenant. It says in Hebrews 9:15-17, *"And for this cause he (Jesus) is the mediator of the new testament, that by means of death, for the redemption of the **transgressions** that were under the first testament, they which are called might receive the promise of eternal* (life) *inheritance (John 3:16-22). For where a testament is, there must also of necessity be the death of the testator. For a testament is of force after men are dead: otherwise it is of no strength all while the testator liveth.* Jesus died for our sins. Jesus is our testator and we have been saved and given the gift of eternal life through Jesus Christ. Who also is the word of God and the truth (John 1:-6; John 14:6).

In order to seek the will of God, we must understand what His will is. Solomon, King of Israel sums it up beautifully in Ecclesiastes 12:13-14, when he says: *"Let us hear the conclusion of the whole matter: Fear* (reverence) *God, and keep his commandments* (be obedient)*: for this is the whole duty of man. For God shall bring every work into judgment, and Every secret thing whether it be good, or whether it be evil."*

God allows us to see that judgment beforehand, the Apostle John said: *"And I saw a great white throne, and him* (God) *that sat on it, from whose face the earth and the heaven fled away; and there was found no place for them. And I saw the dead, small and great, stand before God; and the books were opened: and another book was opened, which is the book of life: and the dead were judged out of those things which were written in the books, according to their works. And the sea gave up the dead which were in it; and death and hell delivered up the dead which were in them: and they were judged every man according to their works. And death and hell were cast into the lake of fire. This is the second death* (eternal separation from God). *And whosoever was not found written in the book of life was cast into the lake of fire* (Revelation 20:11-15; 2 Peter 2:4, 2 Thessalonians 1:5-9). According to the word of God hell is real and in hell are those who are waiting to be judged. *IS YOUR NAME WRITTEN IN THE LAMB'S BOOK OF LIFE?*

Again, pursuit is the act of pursuing, chasing or striding after something or someone; an effort to secure, attain, a quest. The most important word among this definition is the word "effort". Pursuing God takes effort. Something we believers sometimes lack when it comes to God. We would much rather work 40 hours a week for a paycheck than to seek God to reward us for diligently seeking Him. Hebrews 11:5-6 says:

"By faith Enoch was translated that he should not see death; and was not found, because God had translated (Colossians 1:13) *him: for before his translation he had this testimony, that he pleased God. But without faith it is impossible to please him: for he that cometh to God must believe that he is, and that he is a **rewarder** of them that*

diligently seek him."

We are at a grave disadvantage from the beginning if we cannot see, perceive or truly understand who God is and His capacity or power to do all things even now but fail. We fail to believe and understand that God is a rewarder of them that diligently seek him. Some believers now days seem to have only dead faith (James 2:17). Faith that does not respond to God's word, true faith not only believes God but obey what God says. James 2:19 tells us that the devils believe and have enough sense to tremble at the word of God. But we, our minds darken by sin, disregards it.

When pursuing an education, career or money point blank! Just imagine, the work and labor we put forth to achieve our goals. Pursuing God is much more than what we make it out to be. Without **a strong desire** for what we are pursuing. We definitely will not pursue it. And, when we do, it will take much effort to attain it. Pursuing the Lord with our whole heart requires us to search after the Lord and to include him in all our thoughts, feelings, and actions. Its means to take hold of the instructions given us through the word of God and to consider every motion required to come in line with the word of God. For example in Ephesians 5:1-6, and in 1 Corinthians 6:15-20 scriptures tells us that fornicators will not inherit the Kingdom of God, and that our bodies are the temple of the Holy Spirit and that we are not to join our bodies with a harlot (or a whoremonger). But, we allow our emotions and memory to override our knowledge pertaining to God's word. And, rather than resist the temptation to fornicate. We give in to the lust of the flesh. We give in to the flesh rather than to resist (not give in) and walk in the spirit which after God is created in righteousness and true holiness (Ephesians 4:24).

As you continue in the following chapters you will find that love plays a big role in becoming obedient to God. Why? Because, Jesus Christ is the greatest example of what it is to love and please the Father. What it means for us to be a living sacrifice unto God (Romans 12:1-2).

The Apostle Peter gives us instructions as to what we are to do first in 1 Peter 4:1-2, he says:

*"Forasmuch then as Christ hath suffered for us in the flesh, arm yourselves likewise with **the same mind**: for he that hath suffered (enough) in the flesh hath ceased from sin; That he no longer should live the rest of his time in the flesh to the lusts of men, but to the will of God."*

The Apostle Paul then turns around and says in Philippians 2:5-11, *"Let this mind be in you, which was also in Christ Jesus: Who, being in the form of God, thought it not robbery to be equal with God: But made himself of no reputation, and took upon him the form of **a servant**, and was made in the likeness of men: And being found in fashion as a man, **humbled** himself, and **became obedient** unto death, even the death of the cross." Wherefore God also hath highly exalted him, and given him a name which is above every name: That at the name of Jesus every knee should bow, of things in heaven, and things in earth, and things under the earth; And that every tongue should confess that Jesus Christ is Lord, to the glory of God the Father."* And to put the icing on the cake, Paul says: *"Though he were a Son, yet learned he obedience by the things which he suffered; And being made perfect, he became the author of eternal salvation **unto all them that obey him:**"* Spiritual growth requires obedience!

We see in these scriptures so many dimensions to what is required of us to become obedient to the will of God. First of all, we are speaking of pursuing God. We see the mind of Christ who being in the form of God thought it not robbery to be equal with God, but made himself of no reputation, took upon him the form of a servant, humbled himself and became obedient unto death, even the death of the cross. Even though Jesus was the Son of God, scripture says that He learned obedience by the things which he suffered. We spend half our lives suffering simply because we do not want to learn how to obey God?

Suffering does play a role in us learning obedience. Look what the Apostle in 1 Peter 5:6-11 says: *"Humble yourselves therefore under the mighty hand of God, that he may exalt you in due time: Casting all your care upon him; for he careth for you. Be sober; be vigilant; because your adversary* **the devil***, as a roaring lion,* **walketh about, seeking whom he may devour***: whom resist* (not give in to) *stedfast* **in the** **faith,** *knowing that the same afflictions are accomplished in your brethren that are in the world. But the God of all grace,* **who hath called us** *unto his eternal glory by Christ Jesus, after that ye* **have suffered a while***, make you* **perfect** (mature)*, stablish, strengthen, settle you. To him be glory and dominion for ever and ever. Amen."*

We often times suffer as the results of our disobedience to the word of God. And, when we are sick and tired of sin according to 1 Peter 4:1-3 and our lives are half over. We seem to cease then from our sin. Keep in mind that God does chasten those He loves (Hebrews 12:3-11). God corrects our behavior when He allows adverse situations and circumstances to come into our lives (the wiles of the devil). But, God also test our faith through our many trials and tribulations (Romans 5:1-6).

Love on the other hand is the motivating factor to obeying God, intentional obedience, obeying on purpose. For us to walk in love, we must first and foremost truly love God. Scriptures says in 1 John 4:19-21: *"We love him, because he first loved us. If a man say, l love God, and hateth his brother, he is a liar: for he that loveth not his brother whom he hath seen, how can he love God whom he hath not seen? And this commandment have we from him, That he who loveth God love his brother also.*

Love produce or influences positive results. For instance

In Pursuit of God

Jesus says in John 14:23b, speaking to Judas, not Iscariot about how he would manifest himself to them said: *"If a man love me, he will keep my words* (teachings): *and my Father will love him, and we will come unto him, and make our abode* (home) *with him. He that loveth me not keepeth not my sayings: and the word which ye hear is not mine, but the Father's which sent me."*

Jesus then says in John 15:7-12: *"If ye abide in me, and my words abide in you, ye shall ask what ye will, and it shall be done unto you. Herein is my Father glorified, that ye bear much fruit; so shall ye be my disciples. As the Father hath loved me, so have I loved you: continue ye in my love. If ye keep my commandments, ye shall abide in my love; even as I have kept my Father's commandments, and abide in his love. These things have I spoken unto you, that my joy might remain in you, and that your joy might be full. This is my commandment, That ye love one another, as I have loved you."* Is this why we are seeking love in all the wrong places, because we are not abiding in Christ?

What Jesus reveals to us in these passages of scriptures is that God's love is what enables us to become obedience and as a result of our obedience. Joy is produced along with the other fruit of the Spirit. On top of everything else, Jesus promises to answer our prayers and says herein the Father is glorified.

Until we can wrap our minds around the concept of God's love, we will continue to willfully sin (Hebrews 10:26). In spite of our sinful ways, we can become obedient and fully come to understand why God allowed His only begotten Son, Jesus Christ to die for our sinful souls (John 3:16).

Jesus who the scriptures says knew no sin was made sin for us, that we might be made the righteousness of God in Him. And, that while we were yet without strength, Jesus died for the ungodly (John 3:16-17; 2 Corinthians 5:21; Romans 5:6). Paul goes on to say in Romans 15:4:

-1- In Pursuit of God

"For whatsoever things were written aforetime were written for our learning, that we through patience and comfort of the scriptures might have hope (Romans 15:4)."

From Genesis to Revelations and everything in between is for our learning to give us hope and a future (Jeremiah 29:11).

In Pursuit of God

__Chapter 2__

The Way of the Transgressor

"Good understanding giveth favour:
but the way of the transgressor is (difficult) *hard."*
Proverbs 13:15

There is a difference between the sinner and the transgressor. The sinner is born into sin (Psalms 51:13) and it is his or her nature to sin. But, the transgressor has a new nature that cannot sin (1 John 3:9) because it is of God. Yet, sin dwells both in the sinner and transgressor's flesh or mortal bodies (Romans 7:19-25). Because the transgressor is born of the Spirit of God and is a child of God he or she no longer has one nature but two. The transgressor has the old and new nature which after God is created in righteousness and true holiness (Ephesians 4:24). Therefore, we are called to walk in the spirit (new nature) so that we will not fulfill the lust of the flesh (old nature) this means we are to be led of God's Spirit and not the flesh (Galatians 5:16-17).

It is obvious that the way of the transgressor is hard simply because of the transgression of God's commands. Scripture in John chapter three speaks about a man who was *"named Nicodemus, a ruler of the Jews: The same came to Jesus by night, and said unto him, Rabbi, we know that thou are a teacher come from God: for no man can do these miracles that thou does, except God be with him. Jesus answered and said unto him. Verily, verily, I say unto thee, Except a man be born again, he cannot see* (understand) *the kingdom of God."*

When a saved person turns away from sin and **completely surrenders to God.** There is a transformation of the heart, their desire for the ways of God now means more to them than the desire of their own pleasure and satisfaction. There is a

17

new birth, a new life! The ability or capacity to obey God and he or she is now able to see, perceive and or understand spiritual things or the spiritual things of God.

When we are saved by faith and is born of the Spirit of God, we are quicken and made alive in Christ or another way of saying it, we become yoked together with Christ and are called to learn and follow Him. In Matthew 11:28-30 Jesus says: *"Come unto me, all ye that labour and are heavy laden, and I will give you rest* (strength). *Take my yoke upon you* (follow), *and __learn of me;__ for I am meek and lowly in heart: and ye shall find rest unto your souls. For my yoke is easy, and my burden is light."* We come to Jesus, but often times find it hard to learn of him simply because we do not set aside the time to read, study and meditate in the word of God. We allow all the distractions of the world to pull our attention from God's word. Rather than do what is necessary for us to grow and mature. It is easier for us to continue walking in the flesh than the spirit.   When we do not surrender our will to God, and allow the Holy Spirit to lead and empower us we remain in the flesh.

When we are born of God's Spirit and has been connected with Christ through the new birth and is not learning of and following Jesus. We must understand that we really are going in the opposite direction. It is what causes us to struggle. Imagine two oxen who are yoked together and one is trying to go in the opposite direction. The one trying to go in the opposite direction is us because we are not following Jesus. When a child of God transgresses the commandments of God, there is a struggle and it is what scripture calls sin and sin is a heavy load.   Sin is a burden and only when we resist the flesh not giving in to its lustful desires will we be able to walk and live in the spirit.

When we do not give in to the lust of our flesh, we are living and walking according to the word or will of God. We are walking in obedience. We are overcoming self, sin and the world.   Jesus did not leave us helpless. We have been given the Holy Spirit as our comforter and our helper.   The Holy Spirit is the one who enables us or give us the power to overcome our flesh.   When we are disobedience and are sinning against God. We are rebelling against God. We are kicking against the pricks.

Sin is very subtle, which means it is so slight as to be difficult to detect or to describe operating in a hidden usually injurious way; insidious, characterized by or requiring mental acuteness, penetration or discernment. The word of God gives us discernment to recognize our sin. Hebrews 4:12 says:

"For the word of God is quick, and power, and sharper than any twoedged sword piercing even to the dividing asunder of soul and spirit, and of the (body) *joints and marrow, and is a discerner of the thoughts and intents of the heart."*

God's word is able to separate the soul (another name for the mind) from the spirit, and the body, and it is able to discern (make known and help us recognize and understand) the thoughts and the intents of our heart.

Therefore, not having a good understanding of the word of God is what causes so many of us to remain in our sins. Isaiah 28:9-10 says:

"Whom shall he (God) *teach knowledge? And whom shall he make to understand doctrine* (teaching)? *them that are weaned from the milk, and drawn from the breasts. For precept* (a rule) *must be upon precept; percept upon precept; line upon line, line upon line, here a little, and there a little: For every one that useth milk is unskillful in the word of righteousness: for he is a babe* (1 Peter 2:2-3). *But strong meat belongeth to them that are of full age* (mature), *even those who by reason of use have their senses exercised to discern both good and evil* (Hebrews 5:13-14). To be weaned

from the milk of the word, one must discern evil and then choose good by implementing the word of God in their life. Desiring the milk of the word means to learn the word of God and in learning we are now able to then implement the truth in our lives and grow.

Scripture say that we are all taught of God. We would not have come to Jesus had we not been taught of God, and God teaches us through situations and our circumstances. Jesus says:

"No man can come to me, except the Father which hath sent me draw him: and I will raise him up at the last day. It is written in the prophets, And they shall be all taught of God. Every man therefore that hath heard, and hath learned of the Father, cometh to me (John 6:44-45; Matthew 11:28—30).

The way of the transgressor is hard because we do not take the word of God at face value causing us to rationalize. Rationalize means to devise self-satisfying but incorrect reason for one's behavior. We so easily sin because we choose and make choices according to the lust of the flesh and not according to the word or will of God. We allow the law of sin and death to dictate and govern our lives (Romans 8:1-2). Through desire the Spirit of God, who is the Spirit of truth illuminates God's word in our hearts enabling us to see, perceive and or to understand spiritual things or the spiritual things of God. Therefore, desire initiates growth and lust hinders it.

In 1 Peter 2:1-3 it says: *"Wherefore laying aside all malice, and all guile, and hypocrisies, and envies, and all evil speakings, As newborn babes, desire the sincere milk of the word, that ye may grow thereby: If so be ye have tasted that the Lord is gracious."*

We know that the LORD is gracious, but are we willing to give up what we think is good to obey the LORD? We cannot get around the word of God because scripture says faith without works is dead. We must implement (obey) the word of God in our lives in order for our behavior or life to change. The Apostle Peter first of all, tells us to give up these things that are contrary to the will of God. We cannot hold on to ill feelings, deceit, be a hypocrite envying others while gossiping, slandering and backbiting expecting to grow spiritually mature.

Good understanding has a lot to do with us obeying God, as you will learn in the upcoming chapters. You will also learn that God gives us favour because of our obedience and that grace is God's enabling power given to us to overcome sin and any given situation or circumstances we are facing.

When the Apostle Paul sought the Lord three times to remove the thorn from his flesh, Jesus' response in 2 Corinthians 12:9 was: *And he said unto me, My grace is sufficient for thee: for my strength is made perfect in weakness. Most gladly therefore will I* (Paul) *rather glory in my infirmities, that the power of Christ may rest upon me."*

What then is grace? Grace is the enabling power of God. Grace is God's love, mercy and good will toward us unmerited (undeserving) to help us overcome self, sin and any given situation or circumstances we are facing. Whereas, the divine favour of the LORD (merited) is given as a result of our seeking and becoming obedient to the will of God (Proverbs 8:35). The difference between grace and divine favour. Grace takes us from to and divine favour to and on. God through revelation has made this known to me and I am not only walking in God's grace, but I am walking in His favour too!

In Proverbs 2:6; 3:3-4 it says:

"For the LORD giveth wisdom: out of his mouth cometh knowledge and understanding. Let not mercy and truth forsake thee: bind them about thy neck; write them upon the

table of thine heart: So shalt thou find favour, and good
understanding in the sight of God and man.

When we do not fully understand the truth, it will cause us to remain in our sin. John 8:30-32 says:

As he spake these words, many believed on him. Then said Jesus to those Jews which believed on him, If ye continue in my word, then are ye my disciples indeed; And ye shall know the truth, and the truth shall make you free.

The truth will make us free from fear, worry, anxiety and the cares of this world. Jesus says that those who not only believe, but continue in His word are His disciples indeed. To continue means to go on after an interruption, to remain in the same state, capacity or place. What is Jesus saying? Jesus is saying that no matter what comes to interrupt your life. You are to continue in obedience.

The truth is what makes us free. God's word not only makes us free, but it also sanctifies or separates us from the things of the world (John 17:14-19). So many are yet in bondage simply because they do not know the truth and if they know the truth, they are not obeying the truth (Romans 1:18).

Truth is the revealed will of God. It says in Colossians 1:13, *"Who* (God) *hath delivered us from the power of darkness, and hath translated us into the kingdom of his dear Son: In whom we have redemption through his blood, even the forgiveness of sins:"* Who is the Apostle Paul speaking of? The Apostle Paul is speaking of us who are born of the Spirit of God and have already been delivered from the power of darkness and translated into the kingdom of His dear Son and God is calling us to now walk in our deliverance by faith.

The Apostle Paul, who was called Saul before his conversion it says: *"And as he journeyed, he came near Damascus: and suddenly there shined round about him a light from heaven:*

And he fell to the earth, and heard a voice saying unto him, Saul, Saul, why persecutes thou me? And he said, Who art thou, Lord? And the Lord said, I am Jesus whom thou presecutest: it is hard for thee to kick against the pricks. And trembling and astonished said, Lord, what wilt thou have me to do? And the Lord said unto him. Arise, and go into the city, and it shall be told thee what thou must do (Acts 9:3-6). Saul had kick against the prick (a feeling of remorse, regret, or sorrow) and had been ignoring the voice of the LORD and finally he surrendered his will to the LORD and obeyed Him.

The first thing we need to understand is that Saul who was renamed Paul, called Jesus Lord. Scripture says that no man can call Jesus Lord, but by the Holy Spirit. The Apostle Paul in 1 Corinthians 12:3, confirming his born again experience says: *"Wherefore I give you to understand, that no man speaking by the Spirit of God calleth Jesus accursed: and that no man can say that Jesus is the Lord, but by the Holy Ghost."* Saul's conversion was miraculous.

Our conversion is also miraculous. Only we kick against the pricks. We oppose by argument the word of God. Therefore, we must understand that we are engaged in a spiritual war in 2 Corinthians 10:3-6 it says: *For though we walk in the flesh, we do not war after the flesh: (for the weapons of our warfare are not carnal, but might through God to the pulling down of strongholds;) Casting down imaginations, and every high thing that exalteth itself against the knowledge of God, and bringing into captivity every thought to the obedience of Christ. And having in a readiness to revenge* (correct, punish) *all disobedience when your obedience is fulfilled."*

We have to capture every thought and bring our thoughts (minds) into the obedience of Christ. Only then will we be able to overcome self, sin and the evil forces who we have to contend with. It is called spiritual warfare and the battlefield is our minds (Revelation 12:7-12). True obedience can come only through the complete surrender of our will to the will of God. So, the Apostle Paul in Romans 12:1-2 says:

"I BESEECH you therefore, brethren, by the mercies of God, that ye present your bodies a living sacrifice, holy, acceptable unto God, which is your reasonable service. And be not (no longer) *conformed to this world: but be ye transformed by the renewing of your mind, that ye may prove what is that good, and acceptable, and perfect, will of God.*

We can no longer be shaped and molded to this world. We must renew our minds through the word of God and only then will we be able to prove God's good, acceptable, and perfect will for our lives!

___Chapter 3___

Through Forgiveness

"In whom we have redemption through his blood, even the forgiveness of sins.
Colossians 1:14

We who are saved and are born of God's Spirit have been forgiven and must confess when we sin (1 John 1:9). I believe the most sincere cry from the heart is when we acknowledged we were sinners and asked God to forgive and saved us.

Forgiveness is a vital part of our deliverance. Forgiveness is so important that if we do not forgive others. God will not forgive us. These are Jesus' very words and he says: *"For if ye* (we) *forgive men their trespasses, your heavenly Father will also forgive you. But if ye forgive not men their trespasses, neither will your Father forgive your trespasses* (Matthew 6:14-15)." Why then do so many of us hold on to unforgiveness? Maybe we hold on to it knowing God will forgive us, but not really understanding how to forgive others. Or could it be we have not found it in our heart to do so? Not realizing that forgiveness is the beginning of our deliverance. We need to ask God to help us forgive others and move on.

When we repent and turn toward God for help, we are in fact asking God to pardon us. How then are we unable to pardon those who we have not forgiven? The word pardon means, an act of officially saying that someone who was judged to be guilty of a crime or injury will be allowed to go free and will not be punished. "I forgive you" Finding these words in our hearts and meaning them is so hard for many. But when we ask God to forgive us, we are asking him to redeem us from the curse of sin and death. We are asking God to wipe our slates clean. Isaiah speaking for God to the children of Israel spoke unto them and said: *"Wash you, make you clean; put away the evil of your doings from before mine eyes; cease to do evil. Learn to do well; seek judgment, judge the fatherless, plead for the widow. Come now, and let us reason together, saith the LORD: though your sins be as scarlet, they shall be as white as snow; though they be like crimson, they shall be as wool. If ye* **be willing and obedient**, *ye shall eat the good of the land: But if ye* **refuse and rebel,** *ye shall be devoured* (destroyed) *with the sword: for the mouth of the LORD hath spoken* (Isaiah 1:16-20)."

As we can see so many are refusing to come to Jesus and we are seeing their destruction. The pleasure of sin is for a season (Hebrews 11:24-25). But who determine how long that season is? A person drinking with problems over a period of time will and can result in them becoming an alcoholic. Why? Simply because they cannot or will not deal and resolve the issues they are facing in their life. It would not be hard to replace the word drinking with words such as using drugs, having sex, gambling, pornography etc. and adding its ending results. It is sad when we are so blind and deceived by sin, because we refuse to read, study and to obey the word of God. We know about sin but do not fully understand its immediate outcome. Sin separates us from God. Only when sin takes its toll do we become conscious of its destruction and cry for deliverance.

However, sin weight heavy on our soul. But, we can find rest in Jesus (Hebrews 4:9-11), the rest that comes only when we take His yoke (in obedience) upon us and learn of Him. Jesus is the only one able to give us this rest (John 14:27). He is the only one who is able to lift every heavy burden and give us rest from our labor of sin.

This is why prayer is so important when it comes to forgiving others. Through sincere prayer we can receive power and strength to forgive. In Hebrews 4:16 it says: *"Let us therefore come boldly unto the throne of grace that we may obtain mercy, and find grace, to help in time of need.* Sincerely from our heart we can pray and ask God to help us to forgive whoever we are unable to forgive and God will help us. God will heal our hearts as we submit them to Him. We not only have to forgive others, but we have to learn to forgive ourselves. When we do not forgive ourselves we hold on to guilt and shame unnecessarily. Proverbs 28:23 says: *"He that covereth his sins shall not prosper; but whoso confesseth and forsaketh them shall have mercy (1 John 1:9)."* Again, Jesus says in Matthew 11:28-30:

"Come unto me, all ye that labour and are heavy laden, and I will give you rest. Take my yoke upon you, and learn of me; for I am meek and lowly in heart: and ye shall find rest to your souls. For my yoke is easy, and my burden is light."

The word laden is the same word used in 2 Timothy 3:6 which speaks of: *"silly women laden with sins, led away with diver lust:"* Sin is heavy laden!

Many who profess Jesus Christ also fail to really understand what it means to learn of him for when we learn who Jesus is. We learn who we are in Him.   Jesus is God's only begotten Son (John 3:16).   But, we also are sons and daughters of God. God has made a way for us to come into his presence. We can have an audience with Him.   He hears our faintest cry.   He will help and answers our prayers.   The LORD knows how to get our attention and He will.   But let us go boldly unto the Father in prayer making our requests known to Him!   The Apostle Paul says in Philippians 4:9-13 :

"Those things, which ye have both learned, and received, and heard, and seen in me, do: and the God of peace shall be with you. But I rejoiced in the Lord greatly, that now at the last your care of me hath flourished again; wherein ye were also careful (caring), but lacked opportunity. Not that I speak in respect of want: for I have learned, in whatsoever state I am, therewith to be content. I know both how to be abased, and I know how to abound: everywhere and in all things I am instructed both to be full and be hungry, both to abound

and to suffer need. I can do all things through Christ which strengtheneth me."

Whatever we make up our minds to do we can do it through Christ who strengthens us. God have forgiven us. We have forgiven others and ourselves. Now let us move on to perfection. Even though, we could never be perfect here on earth. But, we can follow God's perfect way.

2 Samuel 22:31-33 says:

"As for God, his way is perfect; the word of the LORD is tried (proven)*: he is a buckler* (shield) *to all them that trust in him. For who is God, save the LORD? And who is a rock, save our God? God is my strength and power: and he maketh my way perfect."* Scripture goes on to say:

"There is a way which seemeth right unto a man, but the end thereof are the ways of death (Proverbs 14:12)*."*

In Jesus' instructions He tell us to:

"Enter ye in at the strait gate: for wide is the gate, and broad is the way, that leadeth to destruction, and many there be which go in thereat: Because strait is the gate, and narrow is the way, which leadeth unto life, and few there be that find it (Matthew 7:13-14)."

Pursuing after God each day, confessing and asking God to forgive us when we sin will keep us on the straight and narrow way.   Why? The Bible does not teach that we will not sin. It teaches us not to willfully sin (Hebrews 10:26). We all have sinned and come short of the glory of God. But, God is faithful. He will forgive us when we confess and forsake our sins. The Apostle John in 1 John 1:9-10 tells us:

"If we confess our sins, he is faithful and just to forgive us our sins, and to cleanse us from all unrighteousness. If we

say that we have not sinned, we make him a liar and his word is not in us."

God is not only faithful, but he is just. He not only forgive us our sins, but will cleanse us from all unrighteousness. How many of us truly believe the truth?

I can honestly say I do. I am amaze of how far God has brought me and how much I have grown in the LORD. Words cannot explain how I guard my heart and mind by being very selective of what I allow in my eye and ear gates. I honestly try not to allow any ill feelings to penetrate my heart. As much as possible I bring my thoughts under subjection by not allowing anything not of God to enter my mind or heart with the help of the Holy Spirit.

I am a military veteran of 11 years. When my training in spiritual warfare began it was in October of 1986. It was the first year of my annual military training in the Army National Guard. I remember convoying to our camp ground in Grayling, Michigan. I am sharing one of many testimonies.

Prior to this moment, after I had repented (turned toward God) and was converted (way of thinking changed) in 1976, I was led by the Holy Spirit to make amends with whoever I thought I had hurt, caused any conflict or harm in any way by asking them to forgive me. I remember going on a fast and during my fast I poured my heart out to God. I talked to God about the much pain, injury and disappointment I had experience in my life from a child all the way into adulthood. It was so refreshing and I knew God had forgiven and cleanse my heart.

I grew up in church and at the age of seventeen after high school I went out into the world and was catch up in immortality and needed deliverance from alcohol at the age of twenty-four. I knew God but needed Jesus in my life! In my bondage I cried out to the LORD and He heard my cry. This was part of my prayer:

*"Behold, thou **desirest truth** in the inward parts: and in the hidden part thou shalt make me to know **wisdom**. Purge me with hyssop, and I shall be clean: wash me and I shall be whiter than snow. Make me to hear **joy and gladness**; that the bones which thou hast broken may rejoice. hide thy face from my sins, and blot out all mine **iniquities.** Create in me a **clean heart,** O God; and **renew a right spirit within me**. Cast me not away from thy presence; and take not thy **holy spirit** from me. Restore unto me the joy of thy salvation; and uphold me with thy **free spirit**. Then will **I teach transgressors** thy ways; and **sinners shall be converted unto thee*** (Psalms 51:6-13)."* The LORD has answered my prayer.

My journey with the LORD has been such a humbling experience. All I want now is to please God. I am seeking God for ministry in deliverance.

We were convoying to Grayling, Michigan and I began to see road kill along the freeway. I began to ponder and talk to God in my heart. I grew up such a naive child. So I really could not wrap my mind around them having eyes but not able to see. After a short time I heard the Spirit of the LORD speaking and saying: *"When they see the light* (look at) *it paralyzes them and they are struck.* Likewise, when the enemy sees our light as a result of us walking in truth or in obedience to God's word it paralyzes him. He has a legal right to dwell in darkness because that is his domain. But, when light shines darkness disappear. Light is the absent of darkness. The Holy Spirit then brought to my heart: Matthew 5:14-16 which says: *" Ye are the light of the world. A city that is set on a hill cannot be hid. Neither do men light a candle, and put it under a bushel, but on a candlestick and it gives light unto all that are in the house. Let your light so shine before men, that they may see your good works and glorify your Father which is in heaven."*

-3- Through Forgiveness

We are called to be the reflection of the very God we serve. Are you reflecting God? Are you a shining light in this dark and evil world?

Be careful when you say you know Jesus: *"He that saith, I know him, and keepeth not his commandments, is a liar, and the truth is not in him. But whosoever keepeth his word, in him verily is the love of God perfected: hereby know we that we are in him. He that saith he abideth in him ought himself also so to walk, even as he walked (1 John 2:4-6)."*

Ask yourself this question? Am I a hypocrite? Am I honestly serving God? We have been forgiven of sin to no longer walk in disobedience. Even though sin is subtle, and proceeds from our hearts, it can be seen. 2 Timothy 1:1-7 says:

"This know also, that in the last days perilous times shall come. For men shall be lovers of their own selves, covetous, boasters, proud, blasphemers, disobedient to parents, unthankful, unholy, Without natural affection, truce-breakers, false accusers, incontinent, fierce, despisers of those that are good, Traitors, heady, highminded, lovers of pleasures more than lovers of God; Having a form of godliness, but denying the power thereof: from such turn away. For of this sort are they which creep into houses, and lead captive silly women laden with sins, led away with divers lusts, Ever learning, and never able to come to the knowledge of the truth."

We are all affected by sin either directly or indirectly. We commit sin or someone commit sin against us. Sin as well as love proceeds from the heart. Proceed means to arise, to originate or to result; from the heart.

The Apostle Paul in Romans 5:5 says:

"And hope maketh not ashamed; because the love of God is shed abroad in our hearts by the Holy Ghost which is given

unto us." But Jesus also says:

*"For out of the heart (mind) proceed **evil thoughts**, murders, adulteries, fornications, thefts, false witness, blasphemies: These are the things which defiles a man: but to eat with unwashen hands defileth not a man (Matthew 15:19)."*

David, the King of Israel penned these words in Psalms 119:11, He said:

"Thy word have I hid in my heart, that I might not sin against thee."

David gives us insight into what causes us to sin against God. David says we sin against God because the word is not hidden in our heart. What exactly does it mean to hide the word of God in our hearts? It means to take God's word to heart. It means to memorize or to become familiar with the word of God by reading or studying it. The Holy Spirit will then bring to our remembrance what we need when you need it. When we remember the word of God we store it in our heart (memory or mind) which then **enable our will to act upon it** as we are empowered by the Holy Ghost.

David after repentance was a man after God's own heart and he was able to not sin against God, because he knew and acted upon God's word hidden in his heart rather than sin. David had the love of God also in his heart. In 1 Samuel 13:13-14, Samuel is speaking to King Saul:

"And Samuel said to Saul, Thou hast done foolishly: thou hast not kept the commandment of the LORD thy God, which he commanded thee: for now would the LORD have established thy kingdom upon Israel for ever. But now thy kingdom shall not continue: the LORD hath sought him a man after his own heart, and the LORD hath commanded him to be captain over his people, because thou hast not kept

that which the LORD commanded thee."

Scripture say that David loved the law. In Psalms 119:48, he said:

"My hands also will I lift up (in praise) *unto thy commandments, which I have loved; and I will meditate* (to project in the mind) *in thy statues."*

Again, the motivating factor to obeying the Lord is our love for Him, intentional obedience!

In Pursuit of God

___Chapter 4___

Through Giving

"Give, and it shall be given unto you;
good measure, press down,
shaken together, and running over,
shall men give unto your blossom.
Luke 6:38a

Giving is the first of three spiritual tools given to the believer for the sole purpose of exercising our faith in God. When we take to heart and wrap our minds around the concept of enabling. It will help us understand what enabling is, and its meaning, which means to make (something) possible, practical or easy. Jesus teaches how we are to give and knowing how to give enables us to trust God.

We must begin to learn by doing. Learning to love requires us being patient. Learning to love requires us being kind not envying others, love is not selfish, does not boast or is not proud nor easily offended and so on (1 Corinthians 13:4-13). We learn by doing what we are being taught. We learn to trust God by obeying what Jesus teaches us. I am always open to the Holy Spirit so after I had repent and was pursuing God. I made known to the Lord that I wanted to trust Him, but did not know exactly how. I had experience much disappointment that it was hard for me to wrap my mind around how to trust. It was only a few people I did trust and then was unaware of what I was doing. I knew they loved me and was trustworthy. And, this is the way it should be with the LORD.

During the time I made this known in prayer to God. I heard a still small voice say, "It hard to trust someone you do not know". In other words, the LORD was telling me to get to know Him and I did through His word. I learnt in Genesis how God spoke everything into existence. In the Gospels I was

35

shown Jesus' power to cast out devils and how He fed five thousand souls with two fish and three loaves of bread. He healed the sick, bound up the broken hearted and I saw how Jesus delivered and restored the people of God. In Proverbs, I am obtaining the wisdom of God and the knowledge of how to live, understand and deal with people. In the books of the Prophets, I was shown God's love, mercy and good will toward **His beloved people, along with God's discipline, judgment and chastening**. I can go on and on. When it comes to trusting God, not only do I understand God's power, but I truly understand the commonwealth of the kingdom of God.

Psalms 24:1 says:

"THE EARTH is the LORD'S, and the fullness thereof; the world and they that dwell therein."

"The silver is mine, and the gold is mine, saith the LORD of hosts" Haggai 2:8

"For every beast of the forest is mine, and the cattle upon a thousand hills. I know all the fowls of the mountains: and the wild beasts of the field are mine. If I were hungry, I would not tell thee: for the world is mine, and the fullness thereof." Psalms 50:10-12

Wow! God owns everything! That was my reaction when I read these verses many years ago. We do not belong to ourselves. We have been brought with a price not with silver or gold but with the precious blood of the Lamb who was slain before the foundation of the world (1 Peter 1:18-23).

God has the power to speak into existence whatever He please. I remember as the oldest girl in the family longing for an older sister. Well guess what? God blessed me with my older sister in 2012. We had a cousin to pass and one of my other cousins in Fort Wayne, IN who knew my Sister Micky had mention some folks he knew to her and that her Father had other children beside the ones she already had knowledge of. My cousin was told to give me her telephone number and for me to call and I did. We talked and got to know a little about each other and later that year I went to Fort Wayne for our family reunion on my Mother's side and we met while I was there. I was crying and she was crying. I told her how I had always desired an older sister and how it was such a longing in my heart and God who knew my heart gave me the desire of my heart.

Psalms 37:3-4 tells us to:

" *Trust in the LORD, and do good; so shall thou dwell in the land, and verily thou shalt be fed. Delight thyself also in the LORD, and he shall give thee the desires of thine heart."*

Wow! Words are not sufficient enough for me to explain my feelings that day! I was truly blessed of God and you know what? God is well capable of supplying all of our needs, wants and desires (Philippians 4:19; Proverbs 10:22)!

Giving does require a giving heart. God knows the heart of a giver, a heart that is not selfish. Give means to contribute to some cause. I believe giving is a yardstick to our spiritual growth, and it measures our spiritual maturity. God shapes our attitudes by blessing us according to our obedience. When we give according to the word of God, we say we trust and have faith in you God.

The Apostle Paul let us know also in Romans 12:6-8; 2 Corinthians 9:9-11 that giving is a gift and that God is our supplier he says:

"Having then gifts differing according to the grace that is given us, whether prophecy, let us prophesy according to the proportion of faith; Or ministry, let us wait on our ministering; or he that teacheth, on teaching; Or he that

exhorteth, on exhortation: **he that giveth, let him do it with simplicity (liberality)**; *he that ruleth, with diligence; he that showeth mercy, with cheerfulness. (As it is written, He hath dispersed abroad; he hath given to the poor: his righteousness remaineth for ever. Now he that ministereth seed to the sower both minister bread for your food, and multiply your seed sown, and increase the fruits of your righteousness;) Being enriched in every thing to all bountifulness, which causeth through us thanksgiving to God.*

The Apostle Paul goes on 2 Corinthians 9:7 to instruct us of what to do when we give. I am speaking now of the offering and not the tithe. He says:

"Every man according as he purposeth in his heart, so let him give; not grudgingly, or of necessity: for God loveth a cheerful giver."

The scripture above say that we are to purpose in our heart what to give, to reach a decision of what we are going to give. Then give it not grudgingly or of necessity, because God loves a cheerful giver.

We were just given guidelines for giving from the epistles, now we are going to go to the gospel of Matthew where Jesus is teaching on giving. Jesus gives us clear instructions also on how to give, and the results of our giving. He says:

"Take heed that ye do not your alms before men, to be seen of them: otherwise ye have no reward of your Father which is in heaven. Therefore when thou doest thine alms, do not sound the trumpet before thee, as the hypocrites do in the synagogues and in the streets, that they may have glory of men. Verily I say unto you, They have their reward. But when thou doest alms, let not thy left hand know what the right hand doeth: That thine alms may be in secret: and thy Father which seeth in secret himself shall reward thee openly."

Some leaders of our churches are insisting on lining people up to give according to the amount of money they want them to give. But, Jesus teaches us that giving should be done in secret. Our motive for giving should not be to be seen or to please men. We are not to put on a show. But, we are to give to please God, and when giving is done in faith. God is well pleased because we not only gave in secret but cheerfully knowing that God will openly reward us.

Giving is not always money. It is the giving of our time, and talents. Giving is when we take time out to talk to others about God, how He will help them if they would only learn to trust Him. It is taking someone to the market shopping who does not have an automobile. It is giving information about a job to someone seeking employment. Giving is helping someone who is in need and providing that need. It should not matter what it is because we are the vessels that God uses to pour out His love to others. He knows He can but speak and the needs of those who are seeking Him will be met. It is you and I that will help others come to know Jesus Christ because of the love we show to others in our giving.

God entrusts His resources or riches with believers who have learned or are exercising their gift of giving. Jesus says in Luke 16:10-12:

"He that is faithful in that which is least is faithful also in much: and he that is unjust in the least is unjust also in much. If therefore, ye have not been faithful in the unrighteous mammon, who will commit to your trust the true riches? And if ye have not been faithful in that which is another man's, who shall give you that which is your own?

Jesus often times would answer a question with a question. So, in doing likewise, I will do the same. Who can trust someone who does not trust them? In ministering to the needs of others, we must understand we are instruments of God's righteousness and that the poor always will be with us.

In Pursuit of God

Rather rich or poor. We are to embrace all in our giving trusting God for our supply (Philippians 4:19).

James 2:5 says:

"Hearken, my beloved brethren, Hath not God chosen the poor of this world rich in faith, and heirs of the kingdom which he hath promised to them that love him?

God is calling the poor who are rich in faith and who loves Him. God is going to move on your faith and cause you to prosper in your love and obedience to His word. God wants us to return to Him and to trust Him in these economic times of trouble. If you are a child of God, you are under the economy of God!

Now tithing is different. It is the giving of a tenth of one's gross income weekly, bi-weekly or monthly. The tithe is given and belongs to the LORD. There are those who believe the tithing system ended with the Old Covenant Law and that the tithing system is no longer in effect. Go jump off a building and see if the Law of Gravity has change. The Law Maker, God gave the Law, and God is the only one who can change it, and He has. It is no longer a CARNAL COMMANDMENT, it is a SPIRITUAL LAW.

Right now, I want deal with the New Testament and what Jesus says about tithing. God in His infinite wisdom knew it was not in man's selfish heart to give. So He commanded the blessing through obedience (Deuteronomy 28; Proverbs 10:22). Because of the disobedience of Adam and Eve to not eat from the tree of the knowledge of good and evil all of mankind was cursed. God is still saying to us to choose life or death, to choose blessings or curses. Why? Because, we still have our free will (Genesis 3).

God in His infinite wisdom knew that we all could afford to pay the tithe. It's a matter of faith, obedience, trust, and living wisely. When we really think about the tithe, ten cent from each dollar is not very much to give to God and we could easily live off the other ninety cent if we use it wisely.

In God's fairness, it does not matter how much our gross incomes are; we all are paying the same according to God. Let's look at things from a worldly perspective. In Mark 12:13-17, Jesus was questioned about the tribute (tax) to Caesar by:

...certain of the Pharisees and of the Herodians, to catch him in his words. And when they were come, they say unto him, Master, we know that thou are true, and carest for no man: for thou regardest not the person of men, but teachest the way of God in truth; Is it lawful to give tribute to Ceasar, or not? Shall we give, or shall we not give? But he knowing their hypocrisy, said unto them, Why tempt ye me? Bring me a penny, that I may see it. And they brought it. And he saith unto them, Whose is this image and superscription? And they unto him, Caesar's. And Jesus answering said unto them, Render to Caesar the things that are Caesar's, and **to God the things that are God's***. And they marveled at him"*

Like the Pharisees and Herodians we should not be surprised by the giving of the tithe to God. The tithe belongs to LORD and is a spiritual mark of God. The visible sign we trust Him. God gave marks to identify something or someone (Genesis 4:13-15; Ezekiel 9:6). When we give the tithe we are entrusting our finances to God. God established the tithing system for the purpose of financing the work of ministry on earth and to teach man the fear (reverence) of the LORD (Deuteronomy 14:22-24). What else do we have to give? Absolutely nothing, we own nothing. But, we do give to the LORD honor, praise and glory because it belongs to Him. The tithe honors the sovereign authority and power of God. It is the visible sign of our trust in the LORD. Like the offering when we give our tithes we say to the LORD we honor and trust you. In reality, there is right and wrong, up and down, good and bad. Likewise, there are tithes and taxes.

In Pursuit of God

The tithe is the other side of the coin when it comes to the spiritual realm of the kingdom of God. It is the resource used for the purpose of financing God's ministry here on earth. It is within the economy of God that we pay our tithes to the present day church, the kingdom of God. Malachi 3:8 says:

"Will a man rob God? Yet ye have robbed me. But ye say, wherein have we robbed thee? In tithes and offerings."

The tithe indicates that the offerings came before the tithing system. We see the first sacrifice in Genesis 3:23, and the first offering in Genesis 4:4, and it says:

"And in the process of time it came to pass, that Cain brought of the fruit of the ground an offering unto the LORD. And Abel, he also brought of the firstlings of his flock and the fat thereof. And the LORD had respect unto Abel and to his offering."

The second offering shown in scripture is in Genesis 8:20:

And Noah builded an altar unto the LORD; and took of every clean beast, and of every clean foul, and offered burnt offering on the altar."

Now, we will see the first record of the tithe in Genesis 14:18-20:

"And Melchizedek king of Salem brought forth bread and wine: and he was the priest of the Most High God. And he blessed, him, and said, Blessed be Abram of the most high God, possessor of heaven and earth: And blessed be the most high God, which hath delivered thine enemies into thy hand. And he gave him tithes of all."

The second account of the tithe is recorded in Genesis 28:22, when Jacob vowed to give the tithe of all God blessed him with. Notice this is before the Law of Moses.

The Bible says:

"And Jacob vowed a vow, saying, If God will be with me, and will keep me in this way that I go, and will give me bread to eat, and raiment to put on, So that I come again to my father's house in peace; then shall the LORD be my God: And this stone, which I have set for a pillar, shall be God's house: and of all that thou shalt give me I will surely give the tenth unto thee (Genesis 28:20-22)."

Jacob recognized God as the source of His protection, providence, and partnership. As partners of God, we are given the ability to prosper. Deuteronomy 8:18 says:
"But thou shalt remember the LORD thy God: for it he that giveth thee power to get wealth, that he may establish his covenant which he sware unto thy fathers, as it is this day"

In wrapping this chapter up, Jesus speaks concerning the giving of the tithe in New Testament context. Jesus says:

"But woe unto you, Pharisees! For ye tithe mint and rue and all manner of herbs, and pass over judgment and the love of God: these ought ye to have done, and not to leave the other (tithe) *undone* (Luke 11:42)."

Jesus is saying that the tithe was important and it ought to be done, but judgment and the love of God is equally important and these ought not to be left undone. We say we trust the LORD, but not with our money. We say we believe but do not even want to honor the LORD with our substance which belongs to Him anyway. We are told in Proverbs 3:9-10, to:

"Honour the LORD with (our) *substance, and with the firstfruits of all thine increase: So shall thy barns be filled with plenty, and thy presses shall burst out with new wine."*

The LORD is the same yesterday, today and forever more. The

In Pursuit of God

LORD change not (Malachi 3:6). It is impossible for Him to lie. What have change are the times, culture and the terminology. The LORD is true and faithful. He shall bring to pass every promise made to us. The mandate here in Malachi 3:10 is calling us to return to the LORD. It is calling us to returning to our first love (Revelation 2:4). When a mandate is spoken, we either can heed it or not. We will not be able to say to God that we were not warned. This mandate is not only for the people of God, but for those who are yet in the world.

God before bringing judgment upon a people, nation or individual will always warn and give space to repent (Jonah 1:1-2). The mandate is to bring God's tithe and the offering into the storehouse, the present day church because the tithe honors the sovereign authority and power of God (Malachi 3:7-12). We give the tithe recognizing that our allegiance is to the LORD, and that the earth and all that is within the earth belongs to Him. Therefore, scripture says, we are cursed with a curse even this whole nation (1 Peter 2:9-10).

"Will a man rob God? Yet ye have robbed me. But ye say, Wherein have we robbed thee? In tithes and offerings. Ye are cursed with a curse: for ye have robbed me, even this whole nation. Bring ye all the tithes into the storehouse, that there may be meat (provision) *in mine house, and prove (test) me now herewith, said the LORD of hosts, if I will not open you the windows of heaven, and pour you out a blessing* (Proverbs 10:22), *that there shall not be room enough to receive it. And I will rebuke the* (devil) *devourer for your sakes, and he shall not destroy* (you financially) *the fruits of your ground; neither shall your vine cast her fruit before the time in the field, saith the LORD of hosts. And all nations* (people) *shall call you blessed: Malachi 3:8-12a*

The giving of the tithe develops consistency. God is searching for a people who will be consistent in their walk with the LORD. God is calling us His people to a covenant of faithfulness!

___Chapter 5___

Through Prayer

"Let us therefore come boldly
unto the throne of grace, that we may obtain mercy,
and find grace to help in time of need
Hebrews 4:16

Prayer is the second of three spiritual tools given to the believer for the sole purpose of exercising our faith in God. Jesus says in Matthew 7:7:

"Ask, and it shall be given you; seek, and ye shall find; knock and it shall be opened unto you"

The above scripture tells us exactly what prayer is. Prayer is asking, seeking and knocking. What a wonderful privilege given us to having access to enter God's throne room 24/7. But how many of us really understand the dynamic of prayer, entering beyond the veil to be in the presence of God?

PRAYER MOVES THE HAND OF GOD! Jesus not only explains what prayer is in this scripture, but He also gives us the assurance of answered prayer in Matthew 7:8-11, and says:

"For every one that asketh receiveth, and he that seeketh findeth; and to him that knocketh it shall be opened. Or what man is there of you, whom if his son ask bread, will he give him a stone? Or if he ask a fish, will he give him a serpent" If ye then, being evil, know how to give good gifts unto your children, how much more shall your Father which is in heaven give good things to them that ask him?

Jesus not only assures us of answered prayer. But He also specifies that we should be specific when we pray. In teaching us how to pray Jesus gives us these instructions and guidelines. He says:

45

In Pursuit of God

"And when thou prayest, thou shalt not be as the hypocrites are: for they love to pray standing in the synagogues and in the corners of the streets, that they may be seen of men, Verily I say unto you, They have their reward. But thou, when thou prayest, enter into thy closet, and when thou hast shut thy door, pray to thy Father which is in secret, and thy Father which seeth in secret shall reward thee openly. But when ye pray, use not vain repetitions, as the heathen do: for they think that they shall be heard for their much speaking. Be not ye therefore like unto them; for your Father knoweth what things ye have need of, before ye ask him. After this manner therefore pray ye: Our Father which art in heaven, Hallowed be they name (Matthew 6:7-9).*"*

As with giving we are not to be seen or to put on a show to receive vain glory. Prayer should to be done in the same manner as giving and should be done knowing that our heavenly Father will reward us openly for seeking Him in secret. We don't necessarily have to pray long drawn out prayers or say the same things over and over again. When we pray to the Father we are in fact coming in agreement with Him.   God hears every word we say. Why? First of all, we are told to come boldly unto the throne of grace to obtain mercy and find grace to help in time of need and secondly, the Father knows what we have need of before we ask, so when we pray we are instructed to ask, to seek and to knock which are the three dimensions of prayer. And, as an added assurance the Apostle John in 1 John 5:13-15 tell us:

"These things have I written unto you that believe on the name of the Son of God; that ye may know that ye have eternal life, and that ye may believe on the name of the Son of God. And this is the confidence that we have in him, that, if we ask any thing according to his will, he heareth us: And if we know that he hear us, whatsoever we ask, we know that we have the (requests) *petitions that we* (have asked) *desired of him.*"

This is a very powerful passage of scripture concerning prayer. The Apostle John let us know that we should come believing in the name of Jesus and that we have confidence to know that anything we ask for according to the will of God, we have already because He has heard and have granted our request. We must wait now patiently for its manifestation. When we really believe or are believing God. We will experience the peace of God which surpasses all understanding.

In Philippians 4:6-7 NKJV, the Apostle Paul says:

"Be anxious for nothing, but in everything by prayer and supplication, with thanksgiving, let your requests be made known to God; and the peace of God, which surpasses all understanding, will (keep) *guard your hearts and minds through Christ Jesus."*

When we come to God in sincere prayer making our requests known to Him, believing what we have ask for according to His will. The Apostle Paul tells us that the peace of God that surpasses all understanding will keep or guard our hearts and mind through Christ Jesus. If after coming to God in prayer we are still worried or fearful something has hindered our prayer. We need to search our heart. So many of us do not understand how our sin separates us from God. Even though we are told that nothing shall separate us from the love of God. Yes, I know God is love. But God does love us from a distance. We are what my pastor call distance lovers who are off course or living as the world. Sin separates us from the LORD, but not the love of God. The Prophet Isaiah addresses the backslidden conditions of the Israelites in Isaiah 59:1-2 and says:

"Behold, the LORD's hand is not shortened, that it cannot save; neither his ear heavy that it cannot hear: But your iniquities have separated between you and your God, and your sins have hid his face from you, that he will not hear."

In Pursuit of God

Our prayers are sometimes hindered because of us not being in right standing with God. We must live according to the will of God if we want God to answer our prayers. We must live by faith and not by sight. Living by sight will cause us to remain worried and fearful. We must believe and act on (obey) the word of God.

In prayer we are in relations with God and in that relationship. We will begin to experience God's love and presence as we fellowship with Him. God is a Spirit and His Spirit is the love which fills our hearts as we sincerely come before Him with thanksgiving and praise giving Him adoration. Prayer is where we learn to recognize and hear the voice of God, as He speaks to us in a still small voice.

Prayer also opens our heart to God. Prayer is what **establishes our relationship** with God and helps us to walk in the newness of life. Prayer helps us by us obtaining from God everything we need. We must not only pray, but study the word of God because God speak to us through the written word (2 Timothy 2:15). So the Apostle Paul, in Romans 12:1-2 is first of all, instructing us to present our bodies as living sacrifices unto God, holy and acceptable which is our reasonably service and to no longer be conformed to this world, but to be transformed by the renewing of our minds so that we may prove that good, acceptable, and perfect will of God. When presenting ourselves before God as living sacrifices. We must come before Him with thanksgiving and praise in our hearts understanding that He knows what we have need of before we ask. But, in obedience we are instructed to ask, to seek and to knock in prayer. And, as we pray along with reading and studying the word of God our life will change, as we implemented the truth in our lives. When we refuse to not pray, read or to study diligently the word of God. The results are immature and carnal minded Christians. The local congregation will not reflect Jesus Christ and the love needed to grow the church spiritually will not be present (Ephesians 4:7-16).

-5- Through Prayer

We now see Elijah who goes before the LORD in prayer. I am an Elijah type when it comes to God providing for me. I must trust God every step of the way as seen of God providing for Elijah's needs. In first Kings Chapter nineteen, we see the Prophet Elijah who is running from Jezebel Ahab's wife, who is angry and wants to kill him for the prophets he has slain. He goes to Beer-Sheba where he leaves his servant and goes a day's journey into the wilderness to a juniper tree. Elijah prays to the LORD to die and falls asleep. But the angel of the LORD touches him and tells him to drink a cruse of water and to eat a cake baked on coals. Elijah lies down and goes to sleep again. Then the angel of the LORD comes a second time and touch him to prepare him for the journey to the mount of God in Horeb. Where he fasted on the strength of his last meal forty days and forty nights and scripture says:

"And he came thither unto a cave, and lodged there: And, behold, the word of the LORD came to him and he said unto him, What doest thou here, Elijah? And he said, I have been very jealous for the LORD God of hosts: for the children of Israel have forsaken thy covenant, thrown down thine altars, and slain thy prophets with the sword, and I even, I only, am left; and they seek my life, to take it away.

And he said, Go forth, and stand upon the mount before the LORD. And, behold the LORD passed by, and a great and strong wind rent the mountains, and brake in pieces the rocks before the LORD, but the LORD was not in the wind: and after the wind an earthquake; but the LORD was not in the earthquake: and after the earthquake a fire; but the LORD was not in the fire: and after the fire a still small voice (1 Kings 19:9-12.

Elijah hearing the LORD's voice is then given instructions. We also receive instructions from the LORD as we wait silently to hear His voice or as He speaks to us through the written word as we read and study the word of God. Prayer is the spiritual tool where we talk and God listens and where God talk and we listen. He is able to speak to us or to even show us the answer as we pray, read, and meditate in the word of God. In prayer we connect with God in our relationship with the LORD (John 6:44).

Prayer also is the vehicle we use to receive from God the things we need or want that are tangible and intangible.

What do I mean? Tangible things are the things that can easily be seen or recognized such as a food, shelter, clothing which are all material possessions. Intangible things are things such as wisdom, knowledge, understanding, comfort, strength, healing, and deliverance of which are all unseen and are spiritual in nature. These are some of the examples of things we can receive from God by praying. The tangible we ask God for and the intangible we seek God for and when we are knocking we call it perseverance, which means to continue on even in difficult times.

I understand that there are those of us who may have a productive relationship with the Father. But, for those who may not. I would like to make some suggestions of what should be included or involved in your prayers such as giving adoration with thanksgiving and praise to the Father.

And, if you do not learn anything else, you must learn not to come before God without first confessing and asking God to forgive you of your sins. We want our hearts to be right with God. Our morning prayer should be a time where we ask God to fortify us. Asking to receive the strength we need to help us throughout our day, asking God to also bless others and to meet their needs. In the our evening or at night prayer should be a time when we cast all our cares upon our Father knowing that He cares and loves us. And last but not least, pray without ceasing which means to remain in an attitude of prayer throughout the day. A prayer is just a whisper away!

Spiritual growth is so important in the role of prayer, that we must discipline ourselves by setting aside time to pray. It all comes along with spending quality time with God as we do with others. In our growth progression we need to put forth effort if we are going to grow and become stronger in the LORD. We need to separate ourselves from the things of the world that are a distraction to the will of God and line up our conduct with the expectations of the LORD and we must no longer be conformed to this world, but transformed by the renewing of our mind.

So, the Apostle Paul admonishes us to lay aside every weight and the sin that so easily beset us and for us run with patience the race which is before us, looking unto Jesus who is the author and finisher of our faith. We basically are told two things. One, the need for us to no longer commit sin, and two, the need for us to grow. We grow by nourishing our spirit with the word of God. We grow by obeying the Lord. Our growth depends on our willingness to obey the Lord (who is the Word of God). In Matthew 4:4, Jesus speaking to the devil says:

"It is written, Man shall not live by bread alone, but by every word that proceedeth out of the mouth of God."

In reality, if we neglect eating physical food, the same way we do the reading and the study of God's word. We would be physically weak, and malnourished. Then, we try to understand why we cannot overcome the things that are in the world.

The first link in the cycle of sin is the suggestion. When sin presents itself through a person's suggestion to us or even through our own thoughts caused by a trigger, simulate, or craving. The mind processes our thoughts by searching the memory which then locate past or present experiences concerning the suggestion.   It is what we call memory or recall. If the word of God is not hidden in our heart to counteract our choice of entering into sin and we do not obey, we will yield to the flesh and not the spirit. If the suggestion was extremely harmful or has cause much sorrow. Our desire to please God rather than the flesh will cause us to not enter into the cycle of that particular sin (1 Peter 4:1-2). Often times, even if we have experienced extreme harm or sorrow concerning a particular sin, which we call an addiction. The pleasure we first experience prior to the harm or sorrow will often time override our choice to not sin and we end up giving in to the lust of our flesh.

Suggestion is the link to which we have the ability and the capacity to exercise our power of choice or free will. God did not take away our free will, and we still have the ability or power to exercise it. For an individual who is not renewing the mind through the word of God, it is very difficult for him or her to resist the lust of the flesh. It is easier for them to give in then to resist. James 4:7, gives us ways specifically, how we can break the cycle of sin. James says:

"Submit yourselves therefore to God. Resist the devil (do not give into temptation)*, and he will flee from you. Draw nigh to God and God will draw nigh to you."*

We draw near to God through prayer, praise and worship. Prayer is where we obtain mercy and find grace to help in time of need. Prayer is where we receive our strength. Nehemiah makes known that the joy of the LORD is our strength:

"Then he said unto them, Go your way, eat the fat, and drink the sweet, and send portions unto them for whom nothing is prepared: for this day is holy unto our Lord: neither be ye sorry (sad)*; for the joy of the LORD is your strength* (Nehemiah 8:10)*."*

And, as we enter into God's presence through praise and worship the Psalmist says:

Thou wilt shew me the path of life: in thy presence is the fullness of joy; at thy right hand there are pleasures for evermore (Psalm 16:11)*."*

James 4:8 continue to instruct us by saying:

"Cleanse your hands ye sinners, and purify your hearts ye double minded.

The Apostle James is speaking of the sinner and of those having a double mind. He is referring to the believer who is trying to live both within the kingdom of God and the world (Luke 17:21; Romans 14:17). James says we are unstable in all our ways and our heart needs to be purified. How then do we purify our hearts? We purify our hearts by our hope in the Lord Jesus Christ, who is the hope of glory (Colossians 1:27). 1 John 3:1-3 says:

*"Behold, what manner of love the Father hath bestowed upon us that we should be called the sons of God: therefore the world knoweth us not, because it knew him not. Beloved, now are we the sons of God, and it doth not yet appear what we shall be: but we know that, when he shall appear, **we shall be like him**; for we shall see him as he is. And **every man that hath this hope** in him **purifieth himself,** even as **he is pure**."* Our hope is that we shall be like Jesus!

When in prayer we want to come before God with a pure and sincere heart, a heart that truly loves the LORD. Our LORD has promise us answered prayer also through our obedience and says:

"If ye abide in me, and my words abide in you, ye shall ask what ye will, and it shall be done unto you. Herein is my Father glorified, that ye bear much fruit; so shall ye be my disciples (John 15:7-8)."

For our prayer to be effectual we must become obedient. Why? Because we are told to in James 5:16:

*"Confess your faults one to another, and pray one for another, that ye may be healed. The effectual fervent **prayer***

of a righteous man availeth much."

We must become obedient. We are either walking according to the flesh, or according to the Spirit. There are no in between. The power behind our choice to live for Christ is our love for the Lord, and our knowledge and understanding of the word of God that it is true. What is hindering you? What then is hindering you from obeying the Lord? What do you value more than your love for the Lord? These are questions we should ask ourselves. We must realize that a renewed mind is a mind that has been restored. We actually have to be taught again. We have to be taught how to live according to the ways of God. We have to learn how to forgive, how to love, how to trust, how to show mercy, how to show kindness, how to show compassion, how to be patience and how to become content, etc.

The question we must ask ourselves is, am I going to continue walking in the lust of my flesh, or am I going to desire the things of God and become obedient to His word? We can receive power to overcome our sin or disobedience. But, that power will only come through prayer and fasting.

___Chapter 6___

Through Fasting

*"Is it such a fast that I have chosen? a day for a man to afflict
his soul? Is it to bow down his head as a bulrush, and to
spread sackcloth and ashes under him? wilt thou call this a
fast, and an acceptable day to the LORD?*
Isaiah 58:5

Fasting is the third of three spiritual tools given to the
believer for the sole purpose of exercising our faith in God. It
is a discipline of the body with the tendency to humble the
soul. We develop self-control through denial. Fasting is a
divine corrective to the pride of the human heart. It is
instrumental in our obedience to God. It is the denial of self
which humbles the soul. Fasting is the spiritual tool that God
has design for each of us to discipline our body. God in Isaiah
chapter fifty-eight reveals the fast that is an acceptable day to
the LORD. The house of Jacob sought God daily as if they
were righteous in His sight. They forsook the ordinances of
God, yet were seeking God for justice. They approached God
as if they were delighting themselves in Him and their fasting
to God was in vain. The word of the LORD came to Isaiah and
told him to cry loud and spare not, to lift his voice up like a
trumpet and to show God's people their transgression and
sins. A lot of things we do even today in our churches are in
vain and are not pleasing to God. So they asked God these
questions and says:

*"Wherefore have we fast, say they, and thou seest not?
Wherefore have we afflicted our soul, and thou takest no
knowledge?* God responds and says:

*"Behold, ye fast for strife and debate, and to smite with the
fist of wickedness: ye shall not fast as ye do this day, to make
your voice to be heard on high. Is it a fast that I have chosen?
a day for a man to afflict his soul? Is it to bow down his head*

as a bulrush, and to spread sackcloth and ashes under him?
wilt thou call this a fast, and an acceptable day to the LORD?

God now begins to tell His people about the fast required of
Him, He says:

"Is not this the fast that I have chosen? To loose the bands
of wickedness, and to undo the heavy burdens, and to let the
oppressed go free, and that ye break every yoke? Is it not to
deal thy bread to the hungry, and that thou bring the poor
that are cast out to thy house? When thou seest the naked,
that thou cover him; and that thou hide not thyself from thine
own flesh?

Their fast that displeased God was that they were fasting all
for the wrong reasons (Isaiah 58:3-4). The fast we are called
to requires us to deny ourselves and to put the needs of others
before us. We do this by humbly seeking God through fasting
to receive the guidance, direction and resources needed to
minister to others along with ministering to the LORD!

Fasting is what humbles our soul and disciplines our bodies
because humility is the way of life for the believer. Fasting
cause us to humble ourselves before God. But, the devil he
wants us to desire the things of the world and to exalt
ourselves. There is nothing wrong with having pleasure, as
long as it is not sensual. There is nothing wrong with having
material possessions or becoming popular. There is nothing
wrong with us being famous or wealthy. But if it takes us away
from honoring and serving God then it is wrong. God requires
us to humble ourselves so that He can exalt us and not us
ourselves. Apostle Peter in 1 Peter 5:5-11 says:

"Likewise, ye younger, submit yourselves unto the elder.
Yea, all of you be subject one to another, and be clothed with
humility: for God resisteth the proud, and giveth grace to the
humble. Humble yourselves therefore under the mighty hand
of God, that he may exalt you in due time: Casting all your

cares upon him; for he careth for you. Be sober, be vigilant; because your adversary the devil, as a roaring lion, walketh about seeking whom he may devour: Whom resist (James 4:7) steadfast in the faith, knowing the same afflictions are accomplished in your brethren that are in the world. But the God of all grace, who hath called us unto his glory by Christ Jesus, after that ye have suffered a while, make you (mature) perfect, stablish, strengthen, settle you."

Fasting is communing with God. It is a time we set aside to voluntarily refrain from food and/or drink for a time to give us opportunity to give our full attention to God concerning a particular matter. For fasting to be effective sincere prayer should be accompanied to secure an answer from God. Fasting humbles our soul before God and is designed for each of us in the discipline of our bodies and it releases us into the fullness and power of the Holy Spirit's work in our lives, and it brings us to the point of greater health.

Jesus when asked by the disciples of John why His disciples did not fast?

"And Jesus said unto them, Can the children of the bridechamber mourn, as long as the bridegroom is with them? But the days will come, when the bridegroom shall be taken from them, and then shall they fast (Matthew 9:15)?

In Revelations 19:7-9, it let us know that we are the bride of Christ, the church. Therefore, there was no need for Christ's disciples to fast at that time because Jesus was present with them. But now, we are all call to fast, to afflict our souls so that we may humble ourselves before the Father and so that our Father will exalt us in due time (1Peter 5:6).

So, what does the scriptures say about fasting? Jesus in Matthew 6:16-18 says:

"Moreover when you fast, be not as the hypocrites, of a sad

countenance: for they disfigure their faces, that they may appear unto men to fast. Verily I say unto you, They have their reward. But thou, when you fastest, anoint thine head, and wash thy face; That thou appear not unto men to fast, but unto thy Father which is in secret: and thy Father, which seeth in secret, shall reward thee open."

It is not necessary to tell anyone you are fasting, except your husband or wife. Why? 1 Corinthians 7:4-5 says:

"The wife hath not power of her own body, but the husband: and likewise also the husband hath not power of his own body, but the wife. Defraud ye not one the other, except it be with consent for a time, that ye may give yourselves to fasting and prayer; and come together again, that satan tempt you not for your incontinency."

Others can be told politely when asked the reason you are not eating, "I have turned my plate down."

How then do we fast? For the beginner, it will help you to gradually fast by designating a day and begin with a six hour fast, from noon to 6pm, until you are able to do a twelve hour fast from 6am to 6pm. Then continue until you are able to do a twenty-four hour fast from your designated day at 6pm to 6pm the next day. If you are taking medication, your fast time will revolve around your intake of medication. For example, if you choose to fast from 12 o'clock noon to 6 o'clock in the evening and your medication is scheduled at 3 o'clock pm, you would have some soup or pasta, a dish of wholesome vegetables or a baked potato. This is done each time your medication is scheduled during your designated fast day.

During your designated fast if possible, drink distilled or spring water only. Distilled and spring water is better than faucet water because they help draw toxins out of your cells. Always begin and end your fast with prayer. Whenever possible use this time to read and study the word of God, having a specific purpose for fasting. For example, for spiritual understanding, for healing, for deliverance, for guidance and directions, for a loved one to be saved, for financial blessing, wisdom, spiritual growth, or for the main purpose of receiving answer to prayer. If you should end your fast before your designated time, do not feel defeated. Continue each week fasting on your designated day until you have disciplined yourself to fast one complete day. For example, if you would like your fast day to be on Wednesday of each week, your fast would begin on Tuesday at 6pm and it would end Wednesday at 6pm. You may want to consult your doctor before you begin to fast.

Spending time with God is our objective. Remaining in a spirit of prayer throughout the day, making melody in your heart to the LORD, giving thanks always, what we are actually doing is ministering to the LORD. In Luke 2:36-37, it tells us about a widow named Anna, a prophetess who ministered to God night and day with fasting and prayers, it says:

"And there was one Anna, a prophetess, the daughter of Phanuel, of the tribe of Aser: she was of a great age, and had lived with an husband seven years from her virginity; And she was a widow of about fourscore and four years, which departed not from the temple, but served God with fasting and prayers night and day."

We give our full attention to God when we set aside time to read and study the word of God. When we fast and pray we are allowing the Spirit of God to dominate our bodies, and the benefits of fasting is that it humbles the soul and disciplines our bodies. It also purges our spirit and gives force to our prayers. Fasting releases our faith for healing and it brings deliverance. To sum it all up, fasting cleanses our spirit, mind and body and it humbles our soul all at the same time.

In Isaiah 58:8-11, we are told the results of our fast as required of us:

In Pursuit of God

"Then shall thy light break forth as the morning, and thine health shall spring forth speedily: and thy righteousness shall go before thee; the glory of the LORD shall be thy reward. Then shalt thou call, and the LORD shall answer; thou shalt cry, and he shall say, Here I am. If thou take away from the midst of the yoke (Galatians 5:1), *the putting forth of the finger, and speaking vanity; And if thou draw out thy soul to the hungry, and satisfy the afflicted soul; then shall thy light rise in obscurity, and thy darkness be as the noon day: And the LORD shall guide thee continually, and satisfy thy soul in drought, and make fat thy bones: and thou shalt be like a watered garden, and like a spring of water, whose waters fail not."*

Obeying the LORD and seeking a closer walk with Him through the regular discipline of prayer and fasting is worth the reward God has promise us in Isaiah 58:8-11.

-6- Through Fasting

SCRIPTURE REFERENCE TO FASTING

When we fast	Mark 2:16-20 (now)
How to fast	Matthew 6:16-18 1 Corinthians 7:4-5
Fasting humbles the soul	Psalm 35:13
Fasting afflicts the soul	Isaiah 58:5
Gives force to our prayer	2 Chronicles 7:14
Spiritual efficacy of fasting	Mark 9:29
The acceptable fast	Isaiah 58:3-7
Promise/reward for sincere fast	Isaiah 58:8-11
Public fasts	Joel 1:13-14 Joel 2:12-13 James 4:9
Jesus' private fasts	Matthew 4:1; Mark 1:12-13; Luke 4:1-2
Moses	Deuteronomy 9:9; 18
Elijah	1 Kings 19:8
Daniel	Daniel 10:2-3
Esther	Esther 4:15-17

In Pursuit of God

___Chapter 7___

Through Love

"For this is the love of God,
that we keep his commandments:
and his commandments are not grievous."
1 John 5:3

Love requires obedience and obedience requires love. The two cannot be separated. Love is God and God is love. God cannot be separated from love and true love cannot separate us from God. The Apostle John gives us a clear definition of love when he says: "For this is the love of God, that we keep his commandments: and his commandments are not (burdensome) grievous." Love is the motivating factor when it comes to obeying the LORD. One must ask this question? Do I love myself more than God? Only when we deny self are able to obey the LORD. We twisted the truth because "sin is burdensome" and not the commandments. Sin is what weight heavy on our souls.

Sin is heavy laden and Jesus offers us rest from our labor of sin. Jesus came not only to redeem us from sin, but to deliver us from its bondage and to destroy the works of the devil. Jesus in Matthew 11:28-30 says: *"Come unto to me, all ye that labour and are heavy laden, and I will give you rest. Take my yoke upon you, and learn of me; for I am meek and lowly in heart: and ye shall find rest unto your souls. For my yoke is easy, and my burden is light."*

The transgressor's way is hard, which means I am not obedient to God's commands and my way is difficult because of it. We must understand that after coming to Jesus Christ we are instructed to learn of Him, for in learning we learn who we are in Him. In 2 timothy 3:1-7, the Apostle Paul talks about the conduct of men in the last days and says that these are the perilous times that will come among us. He begin to help us identify the conduct of those who are without Christ by making known the behavior of those who are outside of the will of God and are living in the last days. He says: *"For men shall be lovers of their own selves, covetous, boasters, proud, blasphemers, disobedient to parents, unthankful, unholy, Without natural affection, trucebreakers, false accusers, incontinent, fierce, despisers of those that are good, Traitors, heady, highminded, lovers of pleasures more than lovers of God; Having a form of godliness, but denying the power thereof: from such turn away (2 Timothy 3:2-5)."*

The Apostle Paul helps us identify the behavior of those who are not following Jesus Christ and tells us to turn away from them. Why? Because people behavior has a direct effect on those who are not brought up in the nurture and admonition of the LORD, women being called silly. He says:

"For of this sort are they (men) *which creep into houses, and lead captive silly women laden with sins, led away with divers lusts, Ever learning, and never able to come to the knowledge of the truth (2 Timothy 3:6-7)."*

Men as well as women have the responsibility of coming to know Jesus and we must teach our children. When we are not properly taught we will be ever learning and never able to come to the knowledge of the truth, knowing that truth is what make us free whether we are male or female (John 8:30-32).

Only after learning what love is and what love does will we be able to walk in love. So, the Apostle Paul goes on to tell Timothy that:

"All scripture is given by inspiration of God, and is profitable for doctrine (teaching), *for reproof* (to criticize), *for correction* (make right), *for instruction* (how to do something) *in righteousness: That the man of God may be* (mature) *perfect, thoroughly furnished unto good works (2 Timothy 3:16-17)."*

If we would pay close attention to the teachings of the epistles, we would find that they contain informative as well as practical applications of the scriptures taught by Jesus to the Apostles. The Apostle Paul who tells us that Timothy have known the holy scriptures from a child reminds him that they are able to make him wise unto salvation through the faith which is in Christ Jesus. Therefore, the Apostle Paul tells Timothy to:

"Study to show thyself approved unto God, a workman that needeth not to be ashamed, rightly dividing the word of truth (2 Timothy 2:15)."

To study is much more than reading, we actually are dissecting words allowing the Holy Spirit to form word pictures in our mind so that we may understand what the context is saying. We take ownership of God's word when we study. We allow it to penetrate our hearts.

We get a clearer picture of God when we come to understand His love for humanity and the extent He went to save us from our own destruction. Scripture in John 3:16-17 says:

"For God so loved the world, that he gave his only begotten Son, that whosoever believeth in him should not perish, but have everlasting life. For God sent not his Son into the world to condemn the world; but that the world through him might be saved."

What is God saving us from? The sin we inherited from the transgression of Adam. Ephesians 2:1-3 says:

"And you hath he (made alive) *quickened, who were dead in trespasses and sins; Wherein in time past ye walked according to the course of this world, according to the prince of the power of the air, the spirit that now worketh in the children of disobedience: among whom also we all had our* (conduct) *conversation in times past in the lusts of our flesh,*

fulfilling the desires of the flesh and mind; and were by nature the children of wrath, even as others."

All who have been born of God's Spirit and made alive in Christ Jesus no longer has one nature, but two which after God is created in righteousness and true holiness. Therefore, we are commanded to walk in the spirit or in love. What exactly does this mean? It means we are to deny the flesh and walk in the spirit of love or obedience. It means for us to no longer please the flesh, but God through faith in the LORD, Jesus Christ.

Jesus came not to destroy the law, but to fulfill the law and the fulfilling of the law is love. He did not come to abolish the law (Matthew 5:17-18). What does this mean? Jesus came to validate the law. To show that it could be fulfilled by walking in love. Jesus said on these two commandments hang the law and the prophet. Jesus begins to explain who He is after he silenced the Sadducees who say there is no resurrection. Jesus said in Matthew 22:31-32:

"But touching the resurrection of the dead, have ye not read that which was spoken unto you by God, saying, I am the God of Abraham, and the God of Isaac, and the God of Jacob? <u>God is not the God of the dead, but of the living</u>."

Matthew goes on to tell us that one among the multitude when he heard Jesus' response was astonished at the teaching and asked Jesus a question, tempting him, and saying:

"Master, which is the great commandment in the law? Jesus said unto him, Thou shalt love the Lord thy God with all thy heart, and with all thy soul, and with all they mind. This is the first and great commandment. And the second is like unto it, Thou shalt love thy neighbor as thyself. On these two commandments hang all the law and the prophets (Matthew 22:36-40)."

What was Jesus saying? Jesus was saying that the obtaining of the law was contained in these two commandments and in keeping them both the law was fulfilled, the law that governs the Kingdom of God.

The Apostle Paul speaks also about the fulfillment of the law in Galatians 5:1, 13-14 also and says:

"Stand fast therefore in the (freedom) *liberty wherein Christ hath made us free, and be not entangled again with the yoke of bondage* (Romans 6:18). *For, brethren, we have been called unto liberty; only use not* (freedom) *liberty for an occasion to the flesh, but by love serve one another, For all the law is fulfilled in one word, even in this; Thou shalt love thy neighbor as thyself."*

The Apostle Paul further explains our Christian conduct when he says:

"Owe no man any thing, but to love one another: for he that loveth another hath fulfilled the law." Why? *"Love worketh no ill to his neighbor: therefore love is the fulfilling of the law* (Romans 13:8, 10).*"*

He stresses the importance of us loving one another, but first and foremost without God in our hearts. We are unable to love God let alone one another. So it very important to understand the role love plays in our lives. Love is the motivating factor to obeying God. 1 John 5:1-5 says:

Whosoever believeth that Jesus is the Christ is born of God: and every one that loveth him that begat loveth him also that is begotten of him. By this we know that we love the children of God, when we love God, and keep his commandments. For this is the love of God, that we keep his commandments: and his commandments are not grievous. For whatsoever is born of God overcometh the world: and this is the victory that overcometh the world, even our faith. Who is he that overcometh the world, but he that believeth that Jesus is the Son of God?"

We know from scripture that God is love. What we must truly come to understand now is the expression of love and it is explained throughout the epistles of first John.

<u>Expression of Love</u>

- *"And hereby we do know that we know him, if we keep his commandments."*
  1 John 2:3

- *"He that saith, I know him, and keepeth not his commandments, is a liar, and the truth is not in him. But whoso keepeth his word in him verily is the love of God perfected: hereby know we that we are in him.*
  1 John 2:4-5

- *"He that saith he abideth in him ought himself also so to walk, even as he walked."*
  1 John 2:6

- *"He that loveth his brother abideth in the light, and there is none occasion of stumbling in him."*
  1 John 2:10

- *"Love not the world, neither the things that are in the world. If any man love the world, the love of the Father is not in him. For all that is in the world, the lust of the flesh, and the lust of the eyes and the pride of life, is not of the Father, but is of the world,"*
  1 John 2:15-16

- *"We are of God: he that knoweth God heareth us;*
  He that is not of God heareth not us: Hereby
  Know we the spirit of truth, and the spirit of error."
  1 John 4:6

- *"Beloved, let us love one another: for love is of God;*
  and every one that loveth is born of God, and knoweth
  God."
  1 John 4:7

- *"He that loveth not knoweth not God: for God is love."*
  1 John 4:8

- *"In this was manifested the love of God toward us,*
  because that God sent his only begotten Son into the
  world, that we might live through him."
  1 John 4:9

- *"Herein is love, not that we loved God, but that he*
  loved us, and sent his Son to be the propitiation for our
  sins."
  1 John 4:10

- *"Beloved, if God so loved us, we ought also to love one*
  another."
  1 John 4:11

- *"No man hath seen God at any time. If we love one*
  another, God dwelleth in us, and his love is perfected in
  us."
  1 John 4:12

- *"Hereby know we that we dwell in him, and he in us,*
  because he hath given us of his Spirit."
  1 John 4:13

- "And we have known and believed the love that God hath to us. God is love; and he that dwelleth in love dwelleth in God, and God in him."
1 John 4:16

- *"Herein is love made perfect, that we may have boldness in the day of judgment: because as he is, so are we in the world."*
1 John 4:17

- *"There is no fear in love: but perfect love casteth out fear: because fear hath torment. He that feareth is not made perfect in love."*
1 John 4:18

- *"We love him, because he first loved us."*
1 John 4:19

- *"If a man say, I love God, and hateth his brother, he is a liar: for he that loveth not his brother whom he hath seen, how can he love God whom he hath not seen?"*
1 John 4:20

- *"And this commandment have we from him, That he who loveth God love his brother also."*
1 John 4:21

What is love as defined in the word of God? In 1 Corinthians 13:4-8a, the Apostle Paul says:

"Charity (Love is patient) *suffereth long, and is kind; charity envieth not* (love does not envy)*; charity vaunteth not itself* (love does not boast)*, is not puffed up* (is not prideful)*, Doth not behave itself unseemly* (is not rude)*, seeketh not her own* (is not selfish)*, is not easily provoked* (is not easily offended)*, thinketh no evil; Rejoice not in iniquity* (gross injustice)*, but rejoice in the truth; beareth* (deal with) *all*

things, believeth all things, hopeth all things, endureth all things. Charity (Love) never faileth:

If we are to seek God through love we must walk in love. We must demonstrate the love shown to us by serving others as we serve God. It is in serving others that we are of service to God. When we understand the love of God, it will enable us to become obedience in so much as we will put God first in our lives. We will learn to not fulfill the desires of our flesh, but rather we will please God by walking in obedient to His will.

Jesus says in John 13:34-35, to the disciples:

"A new commandment I give unto you, That ye love one another; as I have loved you, that ye also love one another. By this shall all men know ye are my disciples, if ye have love one to another."

The commandment to love one another was ratified, which meant to approve of the love we are to show one another. Instead of loving one another as we love ourselves. He tells the disciples to now love as He has loved them. We are to love one another with the love of God, and not the love we have for ourselves because there are times when we do not treat ourselves well. The love that Jesus is speaking of is unconditional love. Therefore, we are commanded to love God, one another and even our enemies!

Love is produced by the Holy Spirit and is among the other fruit of the Spirit. One important thing to understand about the production of the fruit is that without Jesus Christ, we are unable to produce genuine fruit. Jesus gives a perfect example by using the illustration of the vine and the branches in the gospel of John. Jesus says:

"I am the true vine, and my Father is the (gardener) *husbandman. Every branch in me that beareth not fruit he*

taketh away: and every branch that beareth fruit, he purgeth (prune) *it, that it may bring forth more fruit* (John 15:1-2).*"*

Jesus explains in the above verses, that the Father is the one who cares for us. He is the one who helps us produce fruit by pruning us, so that we will bear or produce the other fruit of the Spirit. Jesus is careful also to explain that if we do not produce fruit. The Father take the branch away because it is good for nothing but to be cast into the fire and burned. John 15:6, is the verse that refute the once saved always saved teaching, and gives us warning in Hebrews 10:26-31 and Romans 11:16-24 against such teaching. The only way we produce fruit is by abiding in Jesus Christ.

He goes on further by saying in John 15:3-6:

"Now ye are clean through the word which I have spoken unto you. Abide in me, and I in you. As the branch cannot bear fruit of itself, except it abide in the vine; no more can ye, except ye abide in me. I am the vine, ye are the branches: He that abideth in me, and I in him, the same bringeth forth much fruit: for without me ye can do nothing."

Jesus uses the illustration of an olive tree in Romans and a vine here to explain to us that if we do not abide in Him, we will not produce fruit. In order to bear or produce fruit, we must abide or remain connect to Him. When a branch is cut from the vine, it no longer is connected to its source of life and nourishment. It will wither and die and is good for nothing but to be cast into the fire and be burned. It does not take a rocket scientist to see what Jesus is saying about those who are not producing fruit because they are not abiding in Him. To abide means to remain or continue; to endure without yielding. Jesus is speaking of obedience. In our obedience we are not to yield to sin. We are to continue in the word because the word is what cleanses us and love is the motivating factor which causes us to obey the LORD!

__Chapter 8__

Through Joy

"This is the day which the LORD hath made;
we will rejoice and be glad in it."
Psalm 118:24

The fruit of the Spirit is produced by abiding in Christ. Jesus says:

"I am the true vine, and my Father is the husbandman (gardener). *Every branch in me that beareth not fruit he taketh away: and every branch that beareth fruit, he purgeth it, that it may bring forth more fruit (John 15:1-2)."*

Jesus lets us know that the Father is the one who cares for us and makes sure we produce fruit. But, we must understand too that we play a vital role in producing fruit by abiding in Jesus and His word in us for we are cleanse by the word spoken to us. Jesus somehow wants to make this clearer so He says again:

I am the vine, ye are the branches: He that abideth in me, and I in him, the same bringeth forth much fruit: for without me ye can do nothing (John 15:5)."

As long as we are connected to the Jesus, we are connected to our source of life and are able to be nourished so we can grow and produce fruit. But if we refuse to nourish ourselves from the vine by not abiding in the word and the word not abiding in us, we disconnect ourselves from Christ and are good for nothing and are cast forth by the Father and withered; and using a metaphor Jesus says men gather the branches and cast them into the fire and they are burned (John 15:6). And for those who are abiding and producing fruit Jesus gives us this promise, He says:

In Pursuit of God

"If ye abide in me, and my words abide in you, ye shall ask what you will, and it shall be done unto you. Herein is my Father glorified, that ye bear much fruit; so shall ye be my disciples (John 15:7-8)." Our relationship with God is through our prayer life. We must ask, seek, and knock for our daily needs (Matthew 6:9-13)!

In John 8:30-32, Jesus is confirming His word:

"Then said Jesus to those Jews which believed on him, If ye continue in my word, then are ye my disciples indeed; And ye shall know the truth and the truth shall make you free."

Jesus is speaking concerning our obedience to His teachings. Whenever we do not give in to temptation, we triumph over our flesh or enemy and gain Victory! Joy comes after Victory! Wait a minute! Where did that Joy come from? The Joy of the LORD is our strength! Joy comes or is produced as the result of our obedience to walking in love. Jesus says if you love me keep my commandments (John 14:15-31) and the prophet Nehemiah says:

"for this day is holy unto our Lord; neither be ye sorry; for the joy of the LORD is your strength (Nehemiah 8:10b)."

Psalm 28:7 goes on to say:

"The LORD is my strength and my shield; my heart trusted in him and I am helped: Therefore my heart greatly rejoiceth; and with my song will I praise him."

There are nine fruit of the Spirit and joy is among them. The fruit of the Spirit are founded in Galatians 5:22-25 and says:

*"But the fruit of the Spirit is **love, joy**, peace, longsuffering, gentleness, goodness, faith, Meekness, temperance: against such there is no law. And they that are*

*Christ's have crucified the flesh with the affections and lusts.
If we live in the Spirit, let us also walk in the Spirit."*

Joy is an outward manifestation of the overflowing of the
love of God in one's life. Jesus in John 15:9-12, reveals that
the production of joy is produce by walking in love which is a
command given by Jesus to His disciples and these scriptures
reveal that joy comes from the inside and is not predicated on
anything on the outside of us. He says:

*"As the Father hath loved me, so have I loved you: continue
ye in my love. If ye keep my commandments, and abide in
my love; even as I have kept my Father's commandments,
and abide in his love. These things have I spoken unto you,
that my joy might remain in you, and that your joy might be
full. This is my commandment, That ye love one another, as I
have loved you."*

We are specifically being told by Jesus that joy comes as the
result of loving one another or walking in love. I began
chapter seven with the statement "obedience requires love and
love requires obedience. How true! Jesus commands us to
love. By love the world will know that we are Jesus' disciples.

Why is Jesus commanding us to walk in love? Love is
walking in relationship with God, one another and even our
enemies, whereas the world focus is on things and not on
relationships. The Apostle John tells us in 1 John 2:15 to:

*"Love not the world, neither the things that are in the
world. If any man love the world, the love of the Father is not
in him. For all that is in the world, the lust of the flesh, and
the lust of the eyes, and the pride of life, is not of the Father,
but is of the world. And the world passeth away, and the lust
thereof: but he that doeth the will of God abideth for ever."*

We who are truly in Christ Jesus are commanded to love,
period. We are commanded to love God, one another and even

our enemies. Only by abiding in God's love will we be able to walk in obedience to the commandment to love. Love is the royal law. It is the law that governs our hearts. God at this present time is ruling and reigning in the hearts of His people through obedience. The Apostle James in James 2:8-11 says:

If you fulfill the royal law according to the scripture, Thou shalt love thy neighbor as thyself, ye do well. But if ye have respect to persons, ye commit sin, and are convinced of the law as transgressors. For whosoever shall keep the whole law, and yet offend in one point, he is guilty of all. For he that said, Do not commit adultery, said also, Do not kill, Now if thou commit no adultery, yet if thou kill, thou art become a transgressor of the law."

The law that James is speaking of are the Ten Commandments which have been written on our heart through the new birth. Hebrews 10:16-20 tells us:

"For by one offering (Jesus' sacrificial death) *he has perfected for ever them that are sanctified* (separated). *Whereof the Holy Ghost also witness to us: for after that he had said before, This is the covenant that I will make with them after those days, saith the Lord, I will put my laws into their hearts, and in their minds will I write them; and their sins and iniquities will I remember no more. Now where remission of these is, there is* **no more offering for sin***. Having therefore, brethren, boldness to enter into the holiest by the blood of Jesus, By a new and living way, which he hath consecrated for us through the veil, that is to say his flesh.*

This new and living way is calling us to walk in love and in the newness of life. The Apostle Paul addresses sin in the believer's life and says:

"What shall we say then? Shall we continue in sin, that grace may abound (No! We want the favour of God through obedience)*? God forbid. How shall we, that are dead to sin,*

live any longer therein (We are dead to sin and alive in Jesus)? *Know ye not, that so many of us as were baptized into Jesus Christ were baptized into his death? Therefore we are buried with him by baptism into death: that like as Christ was raised up from the dead by the glory of the Father, even so we also should walk in newness of life* (Romans 6:1-4)."

So, our question is what role does joy play in walking in the newness of life? Remember we are told in Nehemiah 8:10 that the joy of the Lord is our strength. It is our strength to endure the faith walk of love and Jesus is our perfect example of obedience. In Hebrews 12:1-2, we are shown a view of Jesus enduring the cross and despising the shame. But before Him was joy! It says:

"Wherefore seeing we also are compassed about with so great a cloud of witnesses, let us lay aside every weight, and the sin which doth so easily beset us, and let us run with **_patience_** *the race that is set before us, Looking unto Jesus the author and finisher of our faith; who for* **the joy** *that was set before him endured the cross, despising the shame, and is set down at the right hand of the throne of God."*

Our destination is heaven! And, in order to reach our destination, we must follow Jesus who is the author and finisher of our faith. We are call to deny self, take up our cross daily and to follow after Jesus and without knowledge of the truth. We have no idea how it is to be done. But God has made available to us the truth of His word and truth reveals the will of God therefore, we are told to study to show ourselves approve unto God, a workman (labourer) that need not be ashamed but rightly dividing the word of truth (2 Timothy 2:15).

The Apostle Paul first of all, tells us to lay aside every weight, and the sin which do so easily beset us. So in our study, we need to understand what weights are and the sin that so easily beset us. Weights are things that hold us back and hinders us from reflecting the LORD such things as smoking, excessive drinking, cursing etc. and I have learnt that besetting sins is the sin that we find so hard to overcome such as sexual sin of fornication, adultery, uncleanness (masturbation) etc. and after we overcome the besetting (entrapping) sin we can then easily overcome others.

Secondly, the Apostle Paul goes on to say in Ephesians 4:20-24:

"But ye have not so learned Christ; If so be that ye have heard him, and have been taught by him, as the truth is in Jesus: That ye put off concerning the former conversation (conduct) *the old* (nature) *man, which is corrupt according to the deceitful lusts; And be renewed in the spirit of your mind; And that ye put on the new* (nature) *man, which after God is created in righteousness and true holiness. "*

The Apostle Paul says that if we have heard and been taught by Jesus, as the truth is in Him we know to put off the conduct of the old sin nature, which is corrupt according to the deceitfulness of lust; and that we are to be renewed in the spirit of our minds (Romans 12:1-2); and for us to put on the new man, which after God is created in righteousness and true holiness.

Paul gives us specific reference to behaviors we are to put off concerning the old man and its conduct. He says to put away lying and to speak the true. He make known that angry is a natural emotion, but we are not to give in to anger and allow it to cause us to sin. In during so we give opportunity for the devil to have a foothold in our lives.

He tells us to not retain anger in our heart, that we must deal with and resolve our anger. Then we are to no longer steal but to work with our hands the thing that is good, that we may have to give to those who need and we also are instructed not to allow any corrupt communication to proceed out of our mouths, but that which is good to the edifying that it may minister grace to those who hear. Stop gossiping, backbiting, whispering, or slandering others by talking against them.

Because the Holy Spirit of God indwells the born again believer. We are now told to not grieve the Holy Spirit of God whereby we are sealed unto the day of redemption. How then do we grieve the Holy Spirit? We grieve the Holy Spirit by yielding to the sin nature when we are lying, angry, stealing, cursing, bitter, are unforgiving and by acts of sexual immorality. We grieve the Holy Spirit by acting out in sinful manners whether in thought or deeds. To grieve is to afflict with deep sorrow. But be mindful, when we walk in love, the joy of the LORD will remain in us, and when we refrain from all these things. We are in obedience and our joy of the LORD will remains full because of it (Ephesians 4:25-32).

The Holy Spirit of God produces joy as we become obedience through love. Love is the motivating factor in our obeying the LORD. What I put before the LORD, I value more! Jesus puts it this way in John 12:24-26:

"Verily, verily, I say unto you, Except a corn of wheat fall into the ground and die, it abideth alone: but if it die, it bringeth forth much fruit. He that loveth his life shall lose it; and he that hateth his life in this world shall keep it unto life eternal. If any man serve me, let him follow me; and where I am, there shall also my servant be (Ephesians 2:6): if any man serve me, him will my Father honour."

We must die to our fleshly desires. So, Jesus says:

"And he said to them all, if any man will come after me, let him deny himself, and take up his cross daily, and follow me. For whosoever will save (keep) his life shall lose it: but whosoever will lose his life for my sake, the same shall save it. For what is a man advantaged, if he gain the whole world, and lose himself, or be cast away (John 15:6)?

In Pursuit of God

We die to self by not giving in to fleshly desires that goes against the word of God. We are to set our affections on the things which are above. The Apostle Paul in Colossians 3:1-10 tells us:

"If ye then be risen with Christ, seek those things which are above, where Christ sitteth on the right hand of God. Set your affection on things above, not on things on the earth. For ye are dead, and your life is hid with Christ in God. When Christ, who is our life, shall appear, then shall ye also appear with him in glory. Mortify therefore your members which are upon the earth; fornication, uncleanness, inordinate affection, evil concupiscence, and covetousness, which is idolatry: for which things' sake the wrath of God cometh on the children of disobedience: In the which ye also walked some time, when ye lived in them. But now ye also put off all these; anger, wrath, malice, blasphemy, filthy communication out of your mouth. Lie not one to another, seeing that ye have put off the old man with his deeds; And have put on the new man, which is renewed in knowledge after the image of him that created him:"

These words are not my words but words given by inspiration of God to the Apostles chosen of the LORD to instruct us in living godly lives.

We will never experience joy without the love of God shed abroad in our hearts by the Holy Ghost (Romans 5:5). Joy is the manifestation of overflowing of the love of God in the believer's life. Unlike happiness which surrounds a person situation or circumstance. Joy comes from the inside and is not predicated on anything on the outside. We can have joy in the mist of sorrow. When everything around us is falling apart, the joy of the LORD is our strength!

Epilogue

Bonus Prophetic Teaching
From the Author

Walking in Obedience to God

-Epilogue-

Walking in Obedience to God

"He that saith he abideth in him ought himself also so to walk,
even as he walked."
1 John 2:6

To obey is to comply or to be willing to comply with orders or requests; to be submissive to the will of another. God's people are called to become submissive to the will of God and to become obedient to the Lord, Jesus Christ. The believer is to submit to the commands of the God in whom we say we believe and have faith in.

Obedience requires love and love requires obedience. The affection of our heart should be geared toward God who has created us. The affection of our heart should be toward the true and living God, the creator of all mankind.

A certain lawyer asked Jesus, "Sir, which is the most important command in the laws of Moses?" Jesus replied, "Love the Lord your God with all your heart, soul and mind." This is the first and greatest commandment. The second most important is similar: "Love your neighbor as much as you love yourself." All the other commandments and all the demands of the prophets stem from these two laws and are fulfilled if you obey them. Keep only these and you will find that you are obeying all the others (Matthew 22:35-37)."

Once we begin to understand our adoption and rebirth into the family of God, we will then understand how important it is for us to submit to the will of God. Let us begin with Jesus, the coming Messiah to the children of Israel and their unbelief. The Apostle Paul in Romans 11:1-3, recap the narrative of how Elias came to God against Israel, saying "Lord, they have killed thy prophets, and digged down thine altars; and I am left alone and they seek my life." God had raised up Elias at a time when the children of Israel were erring into idolatry. They were worshiping Baal and God's response to Elias was this: "But what saith the answer of God unto him? I have reserved to myself seven thousand men, who have not bowed the knee to the image of Baal (Romans 11:4)."

Be sure to know that there are those of us who want to tack the Name of Jesus on as if Jesus is to follow us in our sinfulness, rather we following Jesus. God forbid how so quickly we are deceived to believe we can live anyway and be saved. When we continue to do the very things we were saved from without any change in behavior. Did we really receive Jesus in our heart through faith in God (Romans 10:9-10)?

The Apostle Paul goes on to say: "Even so then at this present time also there is a remnant according to the election of grace (Romans 11:5)." The Gentiles were that remnant. It can be proven by going to the Gospel of John in the tenth chapter. Jesus is speaking about those who have come before Him as representatives claiming to be sent by Him. Jesus said they who belong to Him know His voice and a stranger they would not follow. Jesus stresses also that He is the good shepherd and not a hireling who see the wolf coming and flee because the sheep are not His.

Jesus sheep are known and He calls them by name. He says: "I am the good shepherd, and know my sheep, and am known of mine. As the Father knoweth me, even so I the Father and I lay down my life for the sheep. And other sheep I have, (the election of grace) which are not of this fold (Israel): them also I must bring, and they shall hear my voice; and there shall be one fold, and one shepherd (1 John 2:6)." Gentiles are the elect by grace, the one who has been adopted into the family of the promise of Abraham by faith (Genesis 12:1-3).

The Apostle Paul then speaks of a mystery and is speaking concerning the salvation of both the Israelites and the Gentiles. He says: *"For if the casting away of them be the reconciling of the world, what shall the receiving of them be, but life from the dead? For if the firstfruit* (Jesus) *be holy, the lump is also holy: and if the root* (Jesus) *be holy, so are the branches* (Jews and Gentiles). *And if some of the branches* (Israelites) *be broken off, and thou* (Gentiles), *being a wild olive tree, wert* (were) *graffed in among them, and with them partakes of the root* (Jesus) *and fatness of the olive tree; Boast not against the branches. But if thou boast, thou bearest not the root, but the root thee. Thou wilt say then, The branches* (Israelites) *were broken off, that I* (Gentiles) *might be graffed in. Well; because of unbelief they were broken off, and thou standest by faith. Be not highminded, but fear: For if God spared not the* (the Israelites) *natural branches, take heed lest he also spare not thee. Behold therefore the goodness and severity of God: on them severity;* **_but toward thee, goodness, if thou continue in his goodness: otherwise thou also shalt be cut off_** (Romans 11:15-22).*"*

The Apostle Paul is using an olive tree in Romans 11:15-36 to illustrate how the Gentiles have been engrafted into the family of God. Keep in mind that Paul is not only explaining the salvation that was extended to the Gentiles because God had provoked Israel to jealousy, but Paul is also giving warning that we are not to take our salvation lightly and he refutes the once save always saved teaching. The Apostle Paul warns us against this teaching that has caused many to believe they could live any lifestyle and still go to heaven. As we saw in John 15:1-8, Jesus said if we do not bear fruit the Father take the branch away and every branch that does the Father prunes that it may bring forth more fruit (Galatians 5:22-26).

The Apostle Paul turns to the Gentiles in Romans 11:18 and says:

"Boast not against the branches. But if thou boast, thou bearest not the root, but the root thee."

The word bear means, something that is difficult to do or deal with. The root of the olive tree that is representing Israel is Jesus Christ. The Apostle Paul is saying to us that we will have a difficult time dealing with Jesus should we boast against Israel because Jesus will deal with us concerning the natural olive tree, we being of the wild olive tree grafted in. The Apostle Paul corrects the Gentile church who he is warning by saying: *"Thou wilt say then, The branches were broken off, that I might be graffed in."* Then he says: *"Well; because of unbelief they were broken off, and thou standest by faith. Be not highminded, but fear:* (Romans 11:19-20).

The Apostle Paul now reminds the Gentiles not only of God's goodness, but also of His severity. We are always talking about the goodness of God. True God is good! But God's severity also plays a part in life. Severity is God's strict judgment or how God also governs. It is how he maintains a scrupulous standard of behavior or discipline among His people.

The Apostle Paul says:

"For if God spared not the natural branches, take heed lest he also spare not thee. Behold therefore the goodness and severity of God: on them which fell, severity; but toward thee, goodness, if thou continue in his goodness: otherwise thou also shalt be cut off. And they also, if they abide not still in unbelief, shall be graffed in: for God is able to graff them in again (Romans 11:21-23)."

There goes that "once saved always saved" error in teaching. We cannot say we believe Jesus and not keep His command-ments. Period! The devil has been lying to the body of Christ for years now and the result is what we see in some of our churches today. He has been teaching watered down truth and doctrine of men (Colossians 2:18-23; Matthew 15:8-9).

The Apostle Paul further explains the future salvation of the

Israelites that are rejecting Christ, He says: *"For if thou wert (were) cut out of the olive tree which is wild by nature, and were grafted contrary to nature into a good olive tree: how much more shall these (Israelites), which be the natural branches, be grafted into their own olive tree* (Romans 11:24)?

The Apostle Paul now reveals the mystery and tells us why we must remain connected to our source of life, Jesus Christ. He says:

"For I would not, brethren, that ye should be ignorant of this mystery, lest ye should be wise in your own conceits; that blindness in part happened to Israel, until the fullness of the Gentiles be come (it is now) *in. And so all Israel shall be saved: as it is written. There shall come out of Zion the Deliverer, and shall turn away ungodilness from Jacob: For this is my covenant unto them, when I shall take away their sins* (Romans 11:24-27). Jesus Christ is the Deliverer.

The Apostle Paul then specifies why we are ignoring the truth and why we are being deceived by our gifts and calling which are operating in spite of our sin. He says:

"As concerning the gospel, they are (Israel) *enemies for your sakes: but as touching the election* (the Gentiles), *they are beloved for the father's sakes. For the gifts and calling of God are without repentance* (Romans 11:28)."

Our gifts and calling operates through faith. So when we exercise faith, it brings about the results, in spite of our sin. What we are not exercising is our faith for healing and deliverance which calls for obedience to the word of God. Psalms 107:20-21 says:

"He sent his word, and it healed them, and delivered them from their destruction. Oh that men would praise the LORD for his goodness, and for his wonderful works to the children

of men."

We seek out everything else in our bondage rather than the pursuing of God. Why? Because prior to our salvation, we walked in unbelief, so now we must walk believing God. So the Apostle Paul continues by saying:

"For as ye in time past have not believed God, yet have now obtain mercy through their unbelief. Even so have these also now not believed, that through your mercy they also may obtain mercy. For God hath concluded them all in unbelief, that he might have mercy upon all (Romans 11:30-32)."

When we look at Hebrews 3:7-13, the Apostle Paul is warning us about having an evil heart of unbelief and says:

"Wherefore (as the Holy Ghost saith, To day if ye hear his voice, Harden not your hearts, as in the provocation, in the day of temptation in the wilderness: When your fathers tempted me, proved me, and saw my works forty years. Wherefore I was grieved with that generation, and said, They do always err in their <u>heart</u>; and <u>they have not known my ways</u>. So I sware in my wrath, They shall not enter into my rest.) *Take heed, brethren, lest there be in any of you an evil heart of unbelief, in departing from the living God. But exhort one another daily, while it is called To day; lest any of you be hardened through the deceitfulness of sin."*

As we dissect the scriptures above, the Apostle Paul is saying that the heart is evil because of unbelief and that the cause is the results of the deceitfulness of sin which harden the heart and causes us to depart from the living God. If today we hear the voice of the LORD, we are not to harden our hearts, as in the provocation (time of testing), in the day of temptation as in the wilderness, but we are to draw near to God with a true heart in full assurance of faith, having our hearts sprinkle from an evil conscience, and our bodies washed with pure water. Let us hold fast the profession of our faith without wavering;

(for he is faithful that promise;) and let us consider one another to provoke to love and good works. Let us repent and turn to God, forsaking no longer the assembling of ourselves with the saints. But exhorting one another, and so much the more, as we see the day approaching (Hebrews 10:21-25).

We are so quick to learn about how to be blessed, not really understanding that true blessings are the results of our being obedient (Proverbs 10:22; Malachi 3:10). But, we ignore the warnings of disobedience such as the following verses:

"For if we sin willfully after that we have received the knowledge of the truth, there remaineth no more sacrifice for sins, But a certain fearful looking for of judgment and fiery indignation, which shall devour (intended for our enemies) *the adversaries* (Hebrews 10:26-27).*"*

Obedience is better than sacrifice! What does this really mean? When the LORD sent Samuel to anoint Saul to be King over Israel and instructed Saul to obey the voice of the LORD. Samuel prophesy and says:

"Thus saith the LORD of host, I remember that which Amalek did to Israel, how he laid wait for him in the way, when he came up from Egypt. Now go and smite Amalek, and utterly destroy all that they have, and spare them not; but slay both man and woman, infant and suckling, ox and sheep, camel and ass. And Saul gathered the people together, and numbered them in Telaim, two hundred thousand footmen, and ten thousand men of Judah (1 Samuel 15:2-4).*"*

Saul did not obey the word of the LORD. Scripture said that Saul took the King of the Amalekites, Agag alive, but destroyed all the people with the edge of the sword. And, not only did he spare the King of the Amalekites, but the people he was in charge of spared the best of the sheep, and of the oxen, and of the fatling, and of the lambs, and all that was good they did not utterly destroy. The LORD whom watchful eyes see all things speaks to Samuel and says:

"It repenteth me that I have set up Saul to be King: for he is turned back from following me, and hath not performed my commandments. And it grieved Samuel; and he cried (prayed) unto the LORD all night (1 Samuel 15:10-11)."

It goes on to say that the word came to Samuel that Saul was in Carmel, had set up a place, sacrifice to the LORD and now he can be found in Gilgal. When Samuel found Saul in Gilgal, *"Saul said unto him, Blessed be thou of the LORD: I have performed the command of the LORD. And Samuel said, what meaneth then this bleating of the sheep in mine ears, and the lowering of the oxen which I hear (1 Samuel 15:13b-14)?*

Samuel question Saul because in the LORD's command, Saul was told to destroy everything, not to leave anything alive. Saul who was made king and placed over the people of God, took King Agag alive, then he allowed the people to take the best and good of the livestock, for the people wanted to make a sacrifice unto the LORD.

"And Saul said unto Samuel. Yea I have obeyed the voice of the LORD, and I have gone the way which the LORD sent me, and have Agag the King of Amalekites, and have utterly destroyed the Amalekites. But the people took of the spoil, sheep and oxen, the chief of the things which should have been destroyed, to sacrifice unto the LORD thy God in Gilgal (1Samuel 15:20-21)."

What does this show us? One, we are to lead by example. Two, you cannot make excuses for others, especially if you have authority over them! It only shows the disloyalty of God's people to God and God's leadership.

Listen to what Samuel says to Saul:

-Walking in Obedience to God-

"And Samuel said, Hath the LORD as great delight in burnt offerings and sacrifices, as in obeying the voice of the LORD? Behold, to obey is better than sacrifice, and to hearken (hear and do) *than the fat of rams. For rebellion is as witchcraft, and stubbornness is as iniquity and idolatry. Because thou hast rejected the word of the LORD, he hath also rejected thee from being king* (1 Samuel 15:22-23)."

We reject the word of God in our ignorant. The root word for ignorant is ignore, we ignore the word of God, plain and simple. We put our will, before the will of God. Even though Saul confessed his sin and repented (had a change of mind) and told Samuel what caused him to do it which was fear of the people that he obeyed their voice. Saul continues and says:

Now therefore, I pray thee pardon my sin, and turn again with me, that I may worship the LORD (1 Samuel 15:25)."

Samuel said unto Saul:

'I will not return with thee: for thou hast rejected the word of the LORD, and the LORD hath rejected thee from being king over Israel (1 Samuel 15:26)."

When we disobey God, we are in fact rejecting God. To sacrifice is to give up value. To give up something of value or that we value. It could be your time or money. Both of which we are now doing when we say we are serving the LORD. The LORD does not need our time or money. The LORD is calling us to pursue Him with all of our heart. God is calling us to obey Him by being a living sacrifice, holy, and acceptable unto God, which is our reasonable service and we are not to no longer be shaped and molded by this world but transformed by the renewing of our minds that we may prove what is that good and acceptable and perfect will of God (Romans 12:1-2).

God is calling us to lay down our lives, and taking up the life of Christ is God's perfect will.

-Epilogue-

We reject God's word when we do not want to give up this worldly life by remaining immature and carnal. We remain in fear and not in faith. We try to hold on the old man, rather than put on the new man which after God is created in righteousness and true holiness (Ephesians 4:20-32). It is impossible for us to walk in the newness of life without the renewing of our minds with the word of God. God is calling us to lay our lives on the altar, and to take up the life of Jesus Christ which is a life of obedience to the Father. God is calling us to walk in the righteousness which is of faith (Romans 3:20-24). What is the point?

What is the point of us saying that we are serving God, when in fact we are coming to church every Sunday, yet still satisfied in our sin. God does not delight in our disobedience. We must heed to Paul's warnings and comply with the law that governs us in the Kingdom of God. Love, we are to love God, one another and even those who are our enemies.

1 Samuel 15:22b says:

"Behold, *to obey is better than sacrifice, and to hearken* (hear and do) *than the fat of rams.*"

Repent for the Kingdom of God is at hand!

Thanksgiving Prayers

#1

Heavenly Father,

    I thank you for your Love, Joy and Peace. I thank you Father for your Loving Kindness and your Tender Mercies. I thank you for the Power and Strength you give me. I am thankful for you forgiving me of my sins known and unknown. I thank you for your helping me to overcome my shortcomings and faults. I thank you for enabling me to walk according to your will and your way. I thank you for my family, loved ones and friends. Make me to hear your voice and speak to my heart and mind as I go throughout my day. I give praise, honor and glory to your Holy Name because you alone are worthy. In the Name of Jesus I pray! Amen!

#2

Heavenly Father,

I thank and give you Praise. I thank you that I can recognize that you are worthy to receive all Glory and Honor and Praise. I thank you and renew my allegiance to you and pray that the Blessed Holy Spirit would enable me in this time of prayer. I am thankful, Heavenly Father that you sent the Lord Jesus Christ, your Son into the world to die as my substitute. I am thankful that the Lord Jesus Christ came as my representative and that through Him you have completely forgiven me;   you have birth me into your family; you have assumed all responsibility for me; you have given me Eternal Life; you have given me the Perfect Righteousness of the Lord Jesus Christ so I am now Justified. I am thankful for all you have done for me. In the Name of Jesus! Amen!

Thanksgiving Prayers

#3

Heavenly Father,

Thank you for opening my eyes and allowing me to see how Great you are and how complete your provision is for this day. I am thankful that the Victory the Lord Jesus Christ won for me on the cross and in His resurrection has been given to me and that I am seated with the Lord Jesus Christ in Heavenly places and I recognize by faith that all unclean, wicked, foul, and evil spirits and satan himself are under my feet. I am thankful that you have given me Power and Authority over every unclean, wicked, foul, and evil spirits and they are subject to me in the Name of the Lord Jesus Christ. I thank you for the Power you have given me to walk upright and pleasing in your sight. Thank you for all of your bountiful blessing Lord. In the Name of Jesus I pray, Amen!

#4

Heavenly Father,

I thank you for allowing me to Worship and give you Praise. I thank you for covering me with the Blood of the Lord Jesus Christ, as my protection. I thank you for helping me to surrender my will completely and unreservedly in every area of my life to you. I thank you for helping me take a stand against all the working of satan that would hinder me in my prayer life. I thank you for giving me the Power to refuse any involvement of satan in my life. satan, I rebuke you I command you in the Name of the Lord Jesus to leave my presence with all your demons. I Plea the Blood of Jesus against you, you have no power or authority over me. I thank you Father for helping me to live my life pleasing to you. Give me the courage to say no to all that is not pleasing to you. Give me your love and compassion. Thank you heavenly Father, In the Name of Jesus, Amen!

Prayer Request Form

"Again I say unto you, That if two of you shall agree on earth as touching any thing that they shall ask, it shall be done for them of my Father with is in heaven."
Matthew 18:19

"And this is the confidence that we have in him, that, if we ask any thing according to his will, he heareth us; And if we know that he hear us, whatsoever we ask, we know that we have the petitions that we desired of him."
1 John 5:14-15

Standing on the promises of God!

Prayer Request:

_____

_____

_____

_____

_____

_____

Name_____
                First   Last

Address _____
                        City   State   Zip code

Copy and send to:

Minister Francine E. Shaw
P. O. Box 03600,
Highland Park, MI 48203   95

Contact:

You may send your prayer request to:

C/O Minister Francine E. Shaw
P.O. Box 03600
Highland Park, Michigan 48203

Or

E-mail to:

francineshawministries@yahoo.com

Please include contact information

Thank you!

About the Author

Francine Shaw is an Intercessor, Teacher, and an Evangelist of the New World Community Church, Detroit, Michigan. She is a certified member of International Chaplaincy Training Inc., where she serves as an Ordained Community Chaplain. She has served the LORD for 40 years in ministry of which 10 years were in recovery, deliverance, and spiritual growth and 30 years in training.

Her biblical perspective comes from her knowledge of God, and her actual experience of trusting and walking in the truth of God's Word. She is a Gulf War Veteran, and served in the Army National Guard for 11 years. God used her military training to teach her spiritual warfare, which enabled her to overcoming self, the practice of sin, and the strategies of the devil. Her God given vision is to establish an educational facility for the people of God for the sole purpose of spiritual growth and leadership development.

Francine Shaw contributes her leadership development to the late J. C. Powell, Founder of New World Community Church. The late Bishop Williams Hamilton France Sr., who ordained and trained her in the preaching of the Gospel of Jesus Christ, and Pastor Nathaniel Cotton Sr., who trained her in the Pastoral Ministries. Her present Pastor is Reverend Lernard Goggans Sr. of the New World Community Church. All are Great men of God.

To order additional copies of *The Pursuit of God* or to find more life changing books by *ACTS PUBLISHING,* please contact.

Acts Publishing
P. O. Box 03600
Highland Park, MI 48203
actspublishing@yahoo.com

Or call
(313) 231-6836

Special discounts are available for ministry, academic, retail or fund-raising purposes.

www.ingramcontent.com/pod-product-compliance
Lightning Source LLC
LaVergne TN
LVHW021525080426
835509LV00018B/2674